Shakespeare

Shakespeare

Jeremy Lemmon

HAUS PUBLISHING · LONDON

First published in Great Britain in 2007 by
Haus Publishing Limited
26 Cadogan Court
Draycott Avenue
London SW3 3BX
www.hauspublishing.co.uk

The moral right of the author has been asserted

A CIP catalogue record for this book is available from the British Library

ISBN 978-1-905791-13-2

Typeset in Garamond 3 by MacGuru Ltd
info@macguru.org.uk

Printed in Dubai by Oriental Press

Front cover: Topham Picturepoint

Contents

Foreword

While some aspects of Shakespeare's life are reliably recorded, others
– often the things we most wish to know about – remain frustrat-
ingly uncertain; for these we must rely on traditions, guesswork,
the weighing of probabilities. To the reader who finds this kind
of uncertainty tiresome I can only apologise; and if guesses have
sneaked in disguised as facts I apologise for them too. There is still
debate about when, precisely, and in what order Shakespeare wrote
his plays. I have chosen to adopt the chronology suggested, persuasively but not dogmatically, in the Oxford *Textual Companion*.
This may provide a few surprises: *The Shrew*, for instance, comes a
little earlier than expected. In defiance of chronology, and for the
sake of clarity, I have gathered several non-dramatic works into a
single chapter. Quotations from Shakespeare, and the Act, Scene
and Line numbers, come from the Oxford *Complete Works* (1986).
In a very few instances I have dared to disagree with a reading and
have silently altered it. In all quotations I have modernised the
spelling and occasionally the punctuation too.

I owe a great deal in the way of gratitude, especially to the real
scholars who have written about Shakespeare: it is a privilege to
work in their generous shadow. First among them is, of course, the
great Sir Edmund Chambers, whose gathering together of documentary material is a gift to all biographers. I am indebted to the
late Timothy Wilson Smith for suggesting that I write this book,
and to Barbara Schwepcke for allowing me to do so – and patiently

letting me take my time over it. And special thanks to Christopher Tyerman and James Morwood for their encouragement and help, and to Susan Raleigh-King and Jonathan Rogers for guiding me through the terrors of the computer.

A babe, a child, a shrimp 1564–80

When Shakespeare was born nobody recorded the small event. By the 19th century Stratford-upon-Avon, the country town of his birth, had become a place of pilgrimage: several hundred visitors every year crowded into the house believed to be the birthplace of the Immortal Bard, and great men – Sir Walter Scott, Thomas Carlyle, Sir Henry Irving – cut their names into its latticed window-panes. The Birthplace is still standing, rebuilt and restored, in Henley Street, a stroll away from the river and Clopton Bridge with its sturdy arches. The two parts of the main building were originally two separate, much smaller, houses, and it is generally accepted that it was in one of these (probably, but not certainly, the western house) that in 1564 Shakespeare was born. It must have been late April, since an entry in the parish register records the baptism of 'Gulielmus filius Johannes Shakespere' – William, son of John Shakespeare – on 26 April. A pleasant old tradition has given him an official birthday on 23 April, a date of mythic neatness since it was also to be the day of his death; and it is the feast day of St George, patron saint of England.

Shakespeare was born into comfortable circumstances and at what seemed to be a propitious time. Elizabeth I had been on the throne for six years, and the huge tensions of the preceding reigns seemed to be fading away. Her settlement of the Church was papering over the cracks of religious division. The expensive war with France was over. The purity of the coinage was being restored. Even the fierce winters and lost harvests of the 1550s were just frightening memories. Elizabethan Stratford was a busy town. With a population of between 1,500 and 2,000, it was not as big as Coventry or Worcester, but perhaps a little larger than Birmingham; and it was perfectly placed to be a thriving market centre for livestock and produce and many kinds of manufactured goods; glove-making, the trade of Shakespeare's father, was something of a Midlands speciality. Contemporaries thought Stratford, with its timber-built houses and its many elms,[1] a not-unattractive town.

Shakespeare was a child of his time, growing up in a society that was strongly hierarchical but not immobile. The family was rising in the world. His paternal grandfather, Richard Shakespeare, had been a tenant farmer in the village of Snitterfield, not wealthy but by no means poverty-stricken: when he died his goods were valued at a sum large enough to cover the salary of the Stratford vicar or schoolmaster for nearly two years. By the time of his death his son John had already moved to Stratford, where he set up in business as a glove-maker and whittawer.[2] John seems to have been a resourceful character, ambitious and something of a risk-taker. Apart from his gloves, he dealt in a variety of other goods, particularly, and not legally, in wool.[3] He went in for money-lending too, and was twice brought to court for charging interest at above the legal rate. He also invested in property. In 1556 he was doing well enough to buy his family house in Henley Street, and soon afterwards he married the youngest of the eight daughters of Robert Arden, a prosperous yeoman farmer of Wilmcote and owner of the land worked by Richard Shakespeare. When in 1556 Arden lay dying, he named this youngest daughter an executrix of his will; and he left her a substantial legacy, including an estate, known as Asbyes, in Wilmcote, and a stake in his Snitterfield land. John Shakespeare's marriage to Mary Arden was certainly advantageous to him, but there is no reason to suppose that this was his only consideration. They remained together until his death parted them.

Shakespeare's family lived in a world of craftsmen and traders. Next door to them was a tailor, William Wedgewood, thought to be a bigamist, 'very contentious, proud and slanderous, oft busying himself with naughty matters'.[4] Further along the street was Gilbert Bradley, another glove-maker; one of the Shakespeare sons was probably named after him. Adrian Quiney the mercer had recently moved to the nearby High Street; he and John Shakespeare had once been fined 12 pence for creating an unauthorised dung-heap in Henley Street; the Quineys figure more than once in the story of Shakespeare's life. In Bridge Street lived the tanner Henry Field, whose son Richard was a little older than William Shakespeare; Richard was to become a successful printer in London and to play an important part in establishing Shakespeare's reputation as a poet.

Like several of his neighbours, John Shakespeare was much involved with municipal affairs, a preoccupying business, since Stratford was at that time learning to live with a new civic identity. The religious Guild of the Holy Cross, which had largely administered the town's affairs, had been swept away in 1547, and in 1553 Edward VI, just a week before his death, granted the town a royal charter which in effect made it self-governing. It now had a municipal Corporation with all the paraphernalia of furred gowns and ceremonial mace-bearers, and a hierarchy of Burgesses and Aldermen, with at their head the Bailiff (as the mayor was called). The administrative centre of the town was the Guild's splendid chapel. During the 1560s John Shakespeare was making his way up this Stratford hierarchy.

William was not Mary Shakespeare's first child: two previous babies, both daughters, had failed to survive. It would not be surprising if she watched over this new arrival, her first son, with special tenderness. A popular treatise on child-care advised that, after the birth of her infant, a careful mother should 'anoint all the child's body with oil of acorns, for that is singularly good to confirm, steadfast, and to defend the body from noisome things ...' She should remember to 'set the cradle in such a place that neither the beams of the sun by day nor the moon by night come on the infant'. The baby should be washed 'two or three times in the day' and afterwards 'wiped and handled with gentle and soft linen cloth warmed'. Then the mother should 'lay it on the lap' and tenderly stroke it, 'and so lay it to rest'.[5]

This new baby certainly needed defence from noisome things: when he was less than three months old the plague reached Stratford. The infection had been in London during the previous summer and it spread quickly to become one of the fiercest outbreaks of the century. It was said that in London there were more than 20,000 deaths. In Stratford the figure was about 200 – perhaps 13 per cent of the population. The Shakespeare household was spared, though the danger came near. In August John Shakespeare, now a Burgess, sat with the anxious Council in the garden of the Guild Hall to discuss the crisis: it was safer to meet in the open air.

In 1565 John Shakespeare became an Alderman, with the right to style himself Master Shakespeare and to wear an Alderman's thumb-ring. The family was growing. In 1566 a second boy, Gilbert, was born; and in 1569 a daughter arrived – she was christened Joan, the same name as one of the little girls who had died before William was born; this Joan was the only one of his sisters (there were four in all) to survive into adulthood. In the autumn of the previous year John Shakespeare had reached the peak of the municipal hierarchy: he was elected Bailiff.

One of his duties was to give (or withhold) permission for companies of travelling actors to perform in the town. These troupes were popular, and growing in number; inevitably, like most occupations in Elizabeth's England, they were subject to regulation. A Proclamation of 1559 announced that 'The Queen's Majesty doth straitly forbid all manner Interludes to be played either openly or privately except the same be notified beforehand, and licensed within any city or town corporate, by the Mayor or other chief officers ...' Furthermore, the Mayor (or Bailiff) was charged to be vigilant in permitting no plays which treated of 'matters of religion or of the governance of the estate of the common weal', since such things were the proper concern of 'men of authority, learning and wisdom', and not to be 'handled before any audience, but of grave and discreet persons'.

An Interlude was an entertainment performed during a larger occasion, like a court banquet. In *A Midsummer Night's Dream*, the actors in Peter Quince's little company plan an interlude for *the Duke and Duchess on his wedding day at night*. However, well before Shakespeare's time the word had come to be used for almost any kind of secular play, and an interluder was an actor or entertainer. Since the 19th century historians have used the word to indicate the popular drama of the Tudor period.

Travelling companies could certainly bring trouble: at a performance in Norwich a brawl led to the death of a spectator. And there could be other dangers: in a comedy by Thomas Middleton a foolish mayor is visited by a troupe of interluders, sees nothing odd in the list of plays they offer (*The Whibble*, *The Carwidgeon*, *The Clown and the Cheat*), and gives them permission to perform. He discovers too late that they are 'professed cheaters' who 'take the name of country comedians to abuse simple people', fumble through a few passages from a play, 'and fribble out the rest'. Finally they make off with the spoons.[6]

During John Shakespeare's time as Bailiff two players' companies visited Stratford, the Queen's Men and the Earl of Worcester's Men. Since he authorised payment for both troupes, they must have seemed respectable, though the company of the Queen's Men was in decline. It had for many years been a company of Interluders in the service of the Tudor monarchs (in Edward VI's day they had worked on 'a play of Aesop's Crow, wherein the most part of the actors were birds'); but by 1569 they were no longer welcome at court.[7] Worcester's Men (who received one shilling from the Bailiff) were later to return to Stratford several times. These two companies gave the five-year-old William his first glimpse of the rowdy and colourful world of the professional actor.

The 1570s were, to begin with, good years for John Shakespeare and his family. Though he was never Bailiff again, he remained for some time a significant figure in the Corporation, and he was still buying property. In 1571, when his friend Adrian Quiney was Bailiff, John became chief Alderman. In that same year another daughter, Anne, was born (she was to die before her eighth birthday); and a boy, Richard, William's second brother, was born in 1574.

Although there are no records about the young William's education, as the son of an important townsman he would surely have been sent to the Stratford Grammar School, known as the King's New School because it was during the reign of Edward VI that the old Guild school had been re-established under the control of the Corporation. Schooling was a serious business in Tudor England – something like 300 new schools were founded between 1500 and 1620, 135 of them in Elizabeth's reign. This was partly a matter of the good ordering of the realm; education was seen as a concern of government, which had a hand even in the approving of text-books.[8]

Before being admitted to the Grammar School, the child would have had to learn his letters and Catechism, and it is not wholly impossible that William began his education at home. The fact that both his parents endorsed documents with a mark rather than a signature is not a certain indication that they were unable to write or read; Mary may have been accustomed to using a quill pen.[9] But it is more likely that he was taught at a 'petty school' for small children, perhaps by William Gilbard (or Higgs), a 'very honest, quiet, sober' man who had been under-schoolmaster and took pride in his Latin.[10]

At the age of seven William would have gone on to the main school above the Guild Hall where his father and the Council held their meetings, and when he was ten or eleven he would have reached the Upper School, under the eye of the Schoolmaster himself. Stratford attracted able men for this post. The salary of £20 a year was quite generous (more so than at Warwick; Eton paid £16, with perquisites; the Harrow Statutes, 20 years later, specified just over £26). A house was provided. During Shakespeare's boyhood all the Stratford School-masters had Oxford degrees. In 1575, about the time Shakespeare graduated to the Upper School, the

Shakespeare learned to write in the so-called secretary hand, the practical cursive script which was used by most literate people of his time. To the modern eye it can seem difficult; some letters (*h* and *s*, for example) are particularly unfamiliar. It was gradually being superseded by the clear and beautiful Italian hand, which was used by Elizabeth I. Shakespeare's grand-daughter Elizabeth signed her name in an Italian hand.

Master was Thomas Jenkins, who had come to the school from Warwick; he must have been an unusual man: his father was a servant of Sir Thomas White, the founder of St John's College, Oxford, where Jenkins himself eventually became a Fellow.

At his Stratford school Shakespeare would have moved beyond reading and writing to a serious consideration of language. Studies were wholly concentrated on Latin (some schools added Greek). The pupil learned his rudiments from Lily's *Grammar* (the *Grammatices rudimenta* composed by the founder of St Paul's School, John Colet, and its High Master, William Lily). This famous book was approved by royal decree in order that 'the youth and childhood' of the realm should be 'brought up under one absolute and uniform sort of learning'. It was not intended to be a daunting book: Colet wrote that he had 'left many things out of purpose, considering the tenderness and small capacity of little minds'. The rudiments once mastered, the little minds progressed to more advanced language study. From the best teachers and models – Cicero, Quintilian – they learned the devices of rhetoric, exploring ways of making expression persuasive, elegant or powerful. From Erasmus's *De copia verborum* they discovered 50 ways of saying 'I think it's going to rain'.[11]

There was some reading of plays (in Latin), and it is possible that the children performed extracts from them. Terence was prescribed, and, more cautiously, Plautus – his plays were more improper. Perhaps Shakespeare discovered in passing something about drama, but this was not the explicit purpose of the study. Many schoolmasters must have shared the opinion of Queen Elizabeth's one-time tutor, Roger Ascham (1515–68), who was contemptuous of Terence's plays as plays – trifling tales of 'hard fathers, foolish mothers, unthrifty young men, crafty servants, subtle bawds, and wily harlots'. They were to be studied not for their dramatic qualities but because they were a 'storehouse of pure Latin', and because Terence's words were 'chosen so neatly, placed so orderly, and all his stuff so neatly packed up …'

The children read verse too, especially Virgil and also Ovid, whose poetry was to be so important an influence on Shakespeare's own. His friend and fellow writer Michael Drayton (1563–1631) described the exhilaration of the moment when, after trudging through the earlier studies, he at last discovered poetry. He 'merrily' came to his 'mild Tutor', flung his arms round him, and asked to be told more:

> 'O my dear master! Cannot you (quoth I)
> Make me a Poet? Do it if you can,
> And you shall see I'll quickly be a man.'

Drayton's tutor first gives the child the verse of 'honest Mantuan', the 15th-century Carmelite friar Battista Spagnuoli of Mantua, whose bucolic poems in Latin were essential reading in Elizabethan schools. Then they pass on to Virgil's *Eclogues*, and the little boy, 'scarce ten years of age', feels he has 'mounted Pegasus'.[12] It is pleasant to imagine the child Shakespeare going through the same sort of revelatory experience.

Children like Shakespeare did not, however, have an easy or leisurely time. The Puritan schoolmaster John Brinsley wrote that the school day 'should begin at six', and continue till nine, when a break of a quarter of an hour was permissible, for breakfast, 'or else for the necessity of everyone'. At 11 o'clock there should be a longer break, for dinner, and the children should 'again be all ready and in their places at one, in an instant'. There they should stay, with one more short break, until 'half an hour after five'. After a reading from the Bible, the singing of a psalm, and prayers from the Master, they could be set free. Some recreation might be allowed, but not of a 'clownish' or 'perilous' kind. Punishment should be firm but not cruel; for 'greater faults' it was proper to give 'three or four jerks with a birch, or with a small red willow where a birch cannot be had'. The Master should never chastise his pupils 'in any way as to hurt or endanger them'. The Puritan Brinsley was certain that 'God hath sanctified the rod' and that to spare children 'is to hate them'.[13]

There is no way of knowing whether Shakespeare enjoyed his schooldays. He certainly remembered them. In the plays there are many details drawn from grammar school life; the portrait of the schoolmaster Holofernes in *Love's Labour's Lost* is, not surprisingly, rich in them. This delightful and infuriating pedant enjoys pretty Latin phrases, and he is learned in the ornaments of rhetoric: his *epithets are sweetly varied* – copious in fact (he describes another character as speaking *after his undressed, unpolished, uneducated, unpruned, untrained, or rather unlettered, or ratherest unconfirmed, fashion*). He quotes nostalgically from *good old Mantuan*. His finest and most schoolmasterly moment comes when the country folk present to the courtiers their Interlude of the Nine Worthies. The grandees receive this well-meant effort with remorseless mockery, and Holofernes is not afraid to rebuke them like ill-behaved children. His rebuke (though sadly it has no effect) is both truthful and dignified: *This is not generous, not gentle, not humble*. It is a small sketch of an absurd figure, but it is affectionately drawn.

If Shakespeare did indeed attend the King's New School, he was fortunate in his education. The Tudor system, following the ideals of humanism, aimed to instil godliness (of the approved kind) and to further the studies of good learning; and this education should be open to all.[14] Archbishop Cranmer famously told a group of school commissioners: 'If the gentleman's son be apt to learning let him be admitted; if not apt let the poor man's child, that is apt, enter in his room.'[15] Though Shakespeare was not exactly a poor man's son, his life-journey was remarkable all the same, and his schooling was an important step in it. The yeoman's grandson was becoming part of a literate intelligentsia, in touch with humanist ideas, aware of the resources and possibilities of language.

In 1575, about the time his son was beginning in the Upper School, John Shakespeare bought two more houses in Stratford. Soon afterwards he applied to the College of Heralds for a coat of arms, and the right to the title of Gentleman; the College drew up a preliminary sketch. This was the highest point to which John Shakespeare's aspirations brought him. In 1576 things seemed to change: he was apparently suffering financial difficulties. The granting of arms was an expensive matter, and nothing more was heard of this application for another 20 years. Municipal office also carried expensive obligations. John Shakespeare attended a Council meeting in September – he had not missed a single one since his time as Bailiff; but after this meeting he attended only one more, in 1582. His friends on the Council allowed him to keep his position in name for several years, and they reduced his financial obligations as much as possible, but finally, in 1586, 'for that Master Shakespeare doth not come to halls when they be warned nor hath not done of long time', he lost his place and a new Alderman was appointed.

Family changes did not ease the troubles: in 1579 the little daughter Anne died, and the next year another son, Edmund, was born. William was now the eldest of five children in a family pressed by money troubles. When, in 1580, John Shakespeare, along with more than a hundred others, was summoned to the Court of the Queen's Bench in London to give security to keep the peace, he failed to appear and was given fines amounting to the damaging sum of £40. There were other fines and debts. In the face of these difficulties he resorted to the perilous manoeuvre of alienating land in return for ready money, and soon his wife's inheritance was lost. However, he was never reduced to real poverty: he remained a man of affairs, and 20 years later he was still chasing the hope of retrieving his wife's land through the courts. He did hold on to the property in Henley Street, however; it is likely that by this time the two small houses had been converted into one.

According to some early accounts Shakespeare was forced by his family troubles to leave school before completing his studies so that he could work with his father. This is possible, and it would have been natural; but he was already approaching the age when he would be expected to finish his schooling in the usual way. In any case, his own circumstances were to change utterly before he was out of his teens.

In standing water between boy and man
1580–7?

Towards the end of the 17th century John Aubrey, gathering material for his *Brief Lives*, 'met with old Mr Beeston who knew all the old English poets, whose lives I am taking from him'.[16] This was William Beeston, an old actor whose father, Christopher, had worked with Shakespeare. From this ancient connection Aubrey learned that Shakespeare 'understood Latin pretty well: for he had been in his younger years a schoolmaster in the country'. Aubrey's anecdotage was sometimes inaccurate, but this detail, with its fairly respectable provenance, has invited speculation. Without a licence or a degree, Shakespeare would not have worked in a school, but a clever youth with a recommendation from his own schoolmaster might well be found a post as a tutor in a gentleman's household. In 1579 the Stratford schoolmaster was John Cottam, a Lancashire man whose father's home was not far from land belonging to the wealthy Hoghton family, and when Alexander Hoghton of Lea, a Catholic and a lover of plays, was drawing up his will in 1581, he named in it a certain 'William Shakeshafte now dwelling with me'.[17]

It is a teasing possibility (no more) that this Shakeshafte was the 17-year-old Shakespeare earning his living as 'a schoolmaster in the country', or in some other capacity in this Lancashire household, and that there he came into contact with players. In his will Hoghton 'most heartily' required his friend Sir Thomas

Hesketh of Rufford 'to be friendly' to Shakeshafte, and either take him into service or help him 'to some good master'. Hesketh was also a Catholic, and he kept players – the timber hall at Rufford was well suited to plays and entertainments. Moreover, among his acquaintances was one of the great Elizabethan grandees, the Earl of Derby, who owned a Lancashire property, Lathom House; both Derby and his son Ferdinando, Lord Strange, were patrons of players' companies, and both companies visited Stratford. Strange's troupe later included actors who were to become Shakespeare's friends.

For Catholics like the Hoghtons and the Heskeths – and, conceivably, the Shakespeares too – it was a dangerous time. The religious settlement at the beginning of Elizabeth's reign had set out to achieve at least outward conformity, honouring the 1549 version of the prayer which asked God to grant 'that the course of this world may be so peaceably ordered by thy governance that thy Church may joyfully serve thee in all godly quietness'. But the quietness of true unity was unattainable. The Catholic laity remained, for the most part, discreetly loyal to the Queen and there was at first relatively little persecution. Even the zealous William Allen, who was eventually to become a cardinal and the leader of the unreconciled English Catholics abroad, was able to remain in his Oxford post for more than two years after Elizabeth's accession (it is of incidental interest that he was a Lancashire man – his sister married a Hesketh kinsman). At the other

John Aubrey (1626–97) was an antiquarian, and one of the first Fellows of the Royal Society. He was tireless in ferreting out, recording and preserving curiosities of all kinds. He did much research for the spiteful historian Anthony Wood (1632–95), who in return called him 'maggoty-headed' and 'exceedingly credulous', and claimed that his writing was stuffed with 'fooleries and misinformations'. Aubrey found it almost impossible to organise or complete any of his work. His collection of *Brief Lives*, which was still disordered and 'tumultuarily stitched up' when he died, is a goldmine of irresistible gossip.

end of the religious spectrum, radical Protestants (imprecisely but conveniently lumped together as Puritans) seemed, with their fierce demands for change in both doctrine and practice, a more threatening force for disorder.

However, the fragile compromise which allowed Catholics a quiet life was already failing during the 1560s, even before a trumpet-call from Rome further complicated their situation. Pope Pius V was a remarkable man, who in his early life had been a shepherd before he entered the Dominican order and rose to be a cardinal, Inquisitor General and finally, in 1566, Supreme Pontiff. A spiritual crusader, unyieldingly ascetic (he was later canonised), he had no understanding of compromise or political horse-trading. In 1570 he struck out against the crisis of Christendom by issuing the Bull *Regnans in Excelsis*, which excommunicated and deposed the heretic Queen of England, and relieved her subjects of their duty of allegiance. The English government retaliated by so strengthening the penal laws that from 1571 it seemed impossible to be both a whole-hearted Catholic and a loyal subject: Catholicism was being forced underground.

William Allen set up a seminary at Douai for the training of English priests, and in 1574 the first of 'Allen's men' arrived in England. Within a few years there were a hundred priests from Europe working among the English Catholics. This missionary movement intensified when its organisation came under the control of the Jesuits: it was in the summer of 1580 that the most famous Jesuit missionaries, Robert Persons (1546–1610) and Edmund Campion (1540–81), made their secret landing on the English coast. Their professed purpose was simply to bring the comfort of their ministry to the deprived faithful; they were ordered not to meddle in politics or to speak against the Queen, except in the presence of trusted sympathisers. Campion protested on the scaffold his loyalty to 'Elizabeth your Queen and my Queen, unto whom I wish a long quiet reign with all prosperity'. The

Jesuit poet Robert Southwell (1561–95), who may have had links with Shakespeare, assured the Queen that the loyalty of English Catholics could be relied upon, and that 'what army so ever should come against you, we will rather yield our breasts to be broached by our country's swords, than use our swords to the effusion of our country's blood'.[18] Some of the missionaries may indeed have been genuinely unpolitical; they were certainly heroic. Nevertheless, whether they were conscious of it or not, they were in effect the agents of hostile powers, preparing for the time when a heretic no longer ruled in England. Their hope was not merely to win toleration for Catholics, but to bring England itself back into the fold of Rome: toleration was not a conceivable ideal on either side. Moreover by 1585 England was at war. In the year of the Armada Robert Persons was in Spain working to establish Philip II's claim to the English throne, and Cardinal Allen was thundering against Elizabeth as an unjust usurper, a depraved heretic and the shame of her sex. It is not surprising that her jumpy government should see the English Jesuits as setting up a fifth column.

The dangers reached out towards Stratford. A companion of Persons and Campion on that first secret mission was the invalid Thomas Cottam, brother of the Stratford schoolmaster; he was on his way to visit the family of a fellow-priest, Robert Debdale, when he was arrested; he died on the scaffold in May 1582. Debdale, who came from Shottery, near Stratford, escaped death in 1582, but was tortured and executed at the time of the Babington Plot in 1586. At Lapworth, a few miles from Stratford, Campion was sheltered by Sir William Catesby, father of one of the Gunpowder Plot conspirators. Persons himself, journeying through Warwickshire, was entertained by Edward Arden, who may have been a kinsman of Mary Shakespeare. Arden was hanged at Tyburn, accused of complicity in a plot of his crazy son-in-law John Somerville to shoot the Queen; Somerville died, probably by his own hand, in his prison cell.

There were known Catholics among the Stratford notables; some conformed for a time, and were able to hold office. John Shakespeare may have been one of these discreet conformists, at least until the difficult 1570s, but it could be that a leaning towards Catholicism played a part in his departure from the Corporation. In 1592, during a Privy Council enquiry into recusancy, he was twice named in a list of those who 'come not to church'. It is impossible to know for certain whether the reason officially given for this non-attendance, 'fear of process for debt', was the plain truth or whether he was in fact a recusant; but a strange discovery made nearly two centuries later hints at an answer. In 1757 a workman found, hidden in the roof of the Henley Street house, a little booklet which seemed to be a protestation of faith, a 'spiritual testament', signed by John Shakespeare. The authenticity of this signature can never be tested since the original booklet has vanished; but the text itself was transcribed soon after it was discovered and it turned out to be a document of high Catholic significance, a version of a spiritual testament written by one of the most influential men of the Counter-Reformation, the Cardinal Archbishop of Milan, St Charles Borromeo. Campion and the other missionaries, who visited Borromeo while they were on their journey, are believed to have distributed hundreds of translated copies of his testament among English recusant Catholics. It is not at all unlikely that John Shakespeare was one of them.[19]

Although Shakespeare's father and mother probably had Catholic sympathies, his own beliefs remain hidden. He was baptised and buried by the moderate Protestant church of his time. He certainly knew the Bible – echoes of its language sound through his plays – and he seems to have read in both the officially prescribed Bishops' Bible of 1568 and the popular Geneva Bible (dear to Puritans) of 1560. He knew the Book of Common Prayer too: the language of the Elizabethan Church was thoroughly familiar to him and pervasively influenced his writing. But there is little indication that he knew the Catholic Rheims Bible, of which the New Testament appeared in 1582 and the Old in 1609; it was not a safe book to possess.

However, in the plays there do seem to be reminiscences of Catholic liturgy and beliefs. Some of these are simply related to the context of the play or derived from its source: it is not surprising that in *Romeo and Juliet*, Shakespeare's version of an Italian story, Juliet should speak of going to *evening mass*, or that the Friar, her *ghostly confessor*, should invoke *Holy Saint Francis*. The Catholic echoes in *Hamlet* are more striking, even though they are inconsistent: the Ghost of Old Hamlet is condemned to the prison-house of Purgatory, and rages that he died *unaneled* – that is, without the sacrament of Extreme Unction; and yet young Hamlet is a student at Luther's university of Wittenberg.

An Elizabethan playwright had to bear a wary eye for the censor. The closest Shakespeare came to handling the dangerous material of religious polemic was in a relatively early play, *King John*, where papal authority is an important issue: John's defiance of the Pope was seen as a mirror of Elizabeth's situation. Shakespeare's telling of the story is less violently anti-Catholic than in *The Troublesome Reign of John King of England*, the anonymous play which was probably among his sources. This moderation worried Colley Cibber when he made his own adaptation of Shakespeare's play: he called his version *Papal Tyranny in the Reign of King John*, and it was performed at the time of the Jacobite rebellion of 1745. Cibber thought 'the flaming contest between his insolent Holiness and King John ... so remarkable a passage in our Histories, that it seems surprising our Shakespeare should have taken no more fire at it'. And he wondered whether we should 'go so far for an excuse, as to conclude that Shakespeare was himself a Catholic'.[20] The flaming contest is fought out in the play between the Papal Legate, Cardinal Pandulph, and John, standing for

English independence from the *usurp'd authority* of Rome – his claim is that *under God* he is *supreme head*. The dramatic effect is not simple or clear-cut: both champions are morally ambiguous figures. But Pandulph's great threat is unmistakably pointed and would have been uncomfortably familiar to anyone who remembered Pius V's Bull:

Thou shalt stand curs'd and excommunicate:
And blessed shall he be that doth revolt
From his allegiance to an heretic;
And meritorious shall that hand be call'd,
Canonised and worshipp'd as a saint,
That takes away by any secret course
Thy hateful life.

Some sort of excitement generated by religious debate might have been expected in *Henry VIII*, which Shakespeare wrote in collaboration towards the end of his career; but though the play deals with Henry's divorce from Katherine of Aragon, the huge religious consequences are hardly glanced at. There are a few polemical moments on both sides of the religious divide: Wolsey is attacked as *blind priest*; Anne Boleyn is called *a spleeny Lutheran*. But the central figures are too complex to serve a propagandist purpose. The Catholic Katherine of Aragon and the Protestant Cranmer are both presented as sympathetic, even saintly, figures. There is, however, a curious and suggestive touch, a fleeting reference (perhaps not by Shakespeare) to Sir Thomas More, the Catholic martyr who became the most famous casualty of Henry VIII's breach with Rome. There was no need to mention More at all, since he does not figure in the narrative of the play, and his death came after the events depicted in it; nevertheless he is given a small and significant encomium:

> *He's a learned man. May he continue*
> *Long in his highness' favour, and do justice*
> *For truth's sake and his conscience, that his bones,*
> *When he has run his course and sleeps in blessings,*
> *May have a tomb of orphans' tears wept on him.*

More than half a century after Shakespeare's death, when the anecdotes and traditions were beginning to gather, a clergyman named Richard Davies concluded a brief note about him with a confidently unqualified assertion: 'He died a papist.' Yet during his own lifetime Shakespeare was never called a Catholic. Perhaps, if he was indeed a papist, he was discreet; perhaps he was, like many of his contemporaries, a conforming Protestant who still hankered after the old faith; perhaps at a time of savage division he genuinely preferred peace, order and the moderate Elizabethan church. And perhaps he had no very strong commitment at all. A devout Catholic who loved Shakespeare 'on this side idolatry' suggested a limitation of his dramatist's understanding: 'Shakespeare adulation is something I get a bit edgy about, you know the sort of stuff about sounding every experience of man and all that. Despite all his greatness there is this gaping hole in his make up which Englishmen cannot see. He has no sense of the vitally necessary thing sanctity or holiness. He ... has the trappings of the terminology of the church ... but about as much sense of what sanctity is as Bernard Shaw in *St Joan*.'[21]

If Shakespeare was ever in Lancashire he cannot have stayed there long: he was certainly back in Stratford by the summer of 1582, since in the autumn of that year he was married, and his new wife, Anne Hathaway, was already pregnant. There was clearly some urgency: a licence was entered in the Bishop of Worcester's

Anne Hathaway's cottage

registry on 27 November, allowing the marriage to take place after a single publication of the banns instead of the usual three. The groom is recorded (in Latin) as William Shaxpere and the bride, probably by some clerical confusion, as Anne Whateley of Temple Grafton. The next day a Bond of Sureties was lodged to protect the Bishop and his court from any difficulties arising out of the marriage; two friends of Anne's father stood surety for the bond of £40. In this entry the couple are more recognisable as 'William Shagspere' and 'Anne Hathwey of Stratford maiden'. The licence was issued just in time: Advent began a few days later and ushered in a period of prohibition during which no banns could be published, and this close season lasted until the eighth day of Epiphany, 13 January.

The large family of the Hathaways lived at Hewlands Farm (the substantial house known since the 1790s as Anne Hathaway's Cottage) in Shottery, only about a mile's pleasant walk from Henley Street. Richard Hathaway was already known to the Shakespeares. Anne (or Agnes) was the eldest of the three children of his first marriage, and there were four children from his second. It seems that, although he had Catholic friends, the members of his own family were firmly Protestant: certainly Anne's brother Bartholomew and his sons became churchwardens. Richard died a year before his daughter's marriage, leaving her a small legacy; so Anne was modestly independent, and accustomed to help in the running of a large household, when at the age of 26 she married the 18-year-old Shakespeare.

There is no reason to think the marriage irregular, to see Shakespeare as a youth trapped by his ardour or bullied by a wronged lady's family, or to see Anne as an aging spinster snatching at a last chance. In fact, at that time 26 was the average age for a woman to marry. It might be thought unusual for a husband to be so much younger than his wife, but disparity in age was not in itself uncommon – John Shakespeare was about ten years older than

Mary Arden. Furthermore, Anne's pregnancy was not particularly startling. A solemn contract before witnesses, though probably not recognised as a marriage in law, was seen as binding a couple to their union and lent a liaison some propriety; it was not rare for a bride to be pregnant on her wedding-day.[22] Nevertheless, that this union may not in the end have been closely affectionate is suggested by the fact that throughout Shakespeare's working life Anne never joined him in London, though he did make visits to Stratford. Stephen Dedalus in James Joyce's *Ulysses* puts the uncomfortable question that has troubled admirers of Shakespeare: why is it that during the 34 years of the marriage there is not a single mention of Anne?[23] There is no certain answer; all that can be said is that Shakespeare's silence was not unusual for him; he never wrote explicitly about any of his personal concerns, let alone his personal feelings.

Perhaps the relationship at least began ardently. One love-poem from William to Anne seems to have survived, as Sonnet 145 in the sequence published in 1609. It is quite unlike the other sonnets: it reads as a youthful piece, very different indeed from the bleak and magnificent sonnet that precedes it in the sequence. The lady in this little poem teases her lover by breathing the words *I hate* to him; then, seeing that he is woefully languishing, she sweetly alters the phrase with a charming pendant:

'I hate' from hate away she threw,
And saved my life, saying 'not you'.

The words *hate away* make a graceful play on Anne's family name.[24]

There is no suggestion that Shakespeare's parents disliked the match: for almost the whole period of his working life in London Anne and the children seem to have remained with the Shake-speares in the Henley Street house. The first baby, a daughter, was born in May 1583, just six months after the marriage: the couple named her Susanna. Less than two years later (Shakespeare was not yet 21) the twins, Hamnet and Judith, arrived. They were named after the baker Hamnet Sadler and his wife, Judith, who seem to have been close friends; they were probably Catholics.

After the baptism of the twins on 2 February 1585, Shakespeare's name vanishes from the records, and he does not seem to surface again until 1592. The one tolerable certainty about these much discussed Lost Years is that he must have been earning his living, and the natural likelihood is that he worked for some time with his troubled father; a bright young man skilled in reading and writing would certainly have been helpful to him. Whatever Shakespeare's occupation, his future life may already have been beckoning. In May 1583, just before Susanna was born, a Whitsun entertainment took place in Stratford: the Corporation paid a townsman named Davy Jones to organise it, and it is likely that Shakespeare contributed in some way to it, since Davy Jones was an acquaintance, possibly of a close kind – his first wife had been a daughter of John Shakespeare's old friend Adrian Quiney, and his second was Frances Hathaway, a kinswoman of Anne's. There were other, more significant, opportunities to see plays. During this period Stratford was often visited by travelling companies; in most years there were two, and occasionally there were more.

The status of the players' companies was changing. A statute of 1572 laid down that all 'common players in interludes' must belong to a noble patron; if they could not claim this protection they were to be deemed 'rogues, vagabonds and sturdy beggars'. The penalties were not pleasant: anyone convicted of a 'roguish or vagabond trade of life' should be 'grievously whipped and burnt through the gristle of the right ear with a hot iron of the compass of an inch about'. A third conviction could result in the penalty of death as a felon.[25] Properly constituted companies, however, actually found their position strengthened. The Earl of Leicester's Men, led by James Burbage (1531–97), responded to the new statute by petitioning their great patron to confirm that they were not vagabonds, but indeed his household servants wearing his livery. As the Queen's favourite, Leicester had some influence: in 1574 they were granted a royal patent to exercise 'the art and faculty of playing Comedies, Tragedies, Interludes and stage plays' anywhere throughout the realm of England, provided, of course, that their plays were properly authorised and that they did not perform 'in the time of common prayer' or during a serious outbreak of the plague. Playing was officially labelled an 'art or faculty'; it seems that players were becoming accepted as professionals.[26]

Among the companies Shakespeare would have seen in Stratford were Derby's acting company and Strange's tumblers, Leicester's Men and Worcester's Men, a troupe which included the adolescent Edward Alleyn, soon to be the adored hero of the London playhouses. In 1587 there was a visit by the most important company of the 1580s, the Queen's Men. The company of interluders which had formerly claimed that name had vanished; this one was specially created in 1583 at the command of the Secretary, Sir Francis Walsingham, by creaming players away from other companies to become Her Majesty's Servants and Grooms of the Chamber; among them was the incomparable clown Richard Tarlton, famous for his cross eyes and flat nose as well as for his infinite jest and excellent fancy.

Nobody knows when or why Shakespeare left Stratford. The visiting companies, passing through with their drums and trumpets, may have had something to do with it, by revealing an escape-route to him, or even by offering him a place or the hope of one. Just before they arrived in Stratford the Queen's Men had lost a player, William Knell, stabbed to death by one of his fellows

(Knell's widow later married John Heminges, who was to become one of Shakespeare's close friends). However, the best-loved story about Shakespeare's departure did not concern the players at all. It was first noted by the same Richard Davies who asserted that he 'died a papist', and it was repeated, with variations, by the early biographers. According to this tradition, Shakespeare was caught poaching deer on the land of the powerful Sir Thomas Lucy of Charlecote and whipped for it; after retaliating with an impertinent ballad he was forced to escape from Stratford to avoid severer punishment. Although the story is now often dismissed as legend, not all biographers wholly reject it; indeed it may be based on some fact embedded in Stratford gossip,[27] and it is at least worth consideration, if only as a paradigm of Shakespeare's ambivalent attitude towards established authority. The legend may even imply a darker crisis, since Lucy was an enthusiast in the hunting down not so much of poachers as of Catholics.

The first real biography of Shakespeare was written by Nicholas Rowe (1674–1718) and included in his 1709 edition of the plays. Later editors, including Alexander Pope (1688–1744), Lewis Theobald (1688–1744) and Samuel Johnson (1709–84), added little to Rowe. Shakespearean biography was revolutionised by the work of the great Edmond Malone (1741–1812), whose life of Shakespeare, completed on the basis of his research by James Boswell (1778–1822), son of Johnson's biographer, filled almost a whole volume of the massive 1821 edition of *The Plays and Poems*.

Whatever the cause, it was time to leave Stratford. Life in the Henley Street house cannot have been wholly tranquil. It was home to two families with seven children, the youngest still toddling. John Shakespeare was still in difficulties. There may have been tensions between his sympathies and Bartholomew Hathaway's solid Protestantism. For a young man recently turned 21 and looking to make his fortune, London, the greatest city in England and one of the greatest in Europe, was unquestionably the place to be. Shakespeare certainly knew the success story of his near contemporary Richard Field, who went from Stratford to London in 1579, and was soon bound apprentice to a Huguenot printer and bookseller; when his master died in 1587 Field married the widow and, still in his twenties, took command of a thriving business. It could well be that the same sort of ambition, or dissatisfaction, that led John Shakespeare to leave the Snitterfield farm and make his independent way in Stratford now set his son on the journey to London.

Young ambition's ladder 1587?–92

In 1587 a portent was observed in the night sky, a single star visible between the horns of the crescent moon. Shakespeare may well have seen it from lodgings in London. The date of his arrival there is not known, but it must have been a few years before 1592, since he had already made a name for himself as an actor and writer, probably of several plays, before he became, in that year, the target of a famous attack by another writer. Robert Greene (1558–92) was a remarkable fellow, gifted and quarrelsome – and vividly recognisable in his 'very fair cloak with sleeves of a grave goose-turd green' and with his eccentric hair and beard, 'a jolly long red peak, like the spire of a steeple … whereat a man might hang a jewel, it was so sharp and pendent'. Greene was living a disreputable life in London with his mistress (the sister of a well-known thief) and an illegitimate son hopefully named Fortunatus, when in the summer of 1592 he fell ill after a 'fatal banquet of Rhenish wine and pickled herring';[28] in September he died, penniless and bitter, in the house of a shoemaker.

A few weeks later a pamphlet appeared, allegedly written by Greene and 'published at his dying request'; it was entitled *Greene's Groatsworth of Wit, Bought with a Million of Repentance*. In it he airs his resentment that parasitical players can make their fortunes out of a writer's work, and go about like gentlemen 'of great living' while men of rare wit are 'subject to the pleasures of such rude grooms'. He warns his fellow writers not to trust the players, 'those puppets ... that speak from our mouths, those antics garnished in our colours'. And he singles out for attack a particular player who is actually aspiring to be a writer as well: 'there is an upstart Crow, beautified with our feathers, that with his *Tiger's heart wrapped in a Player's hide*, supposes he is as well able to bombast out a blank verse as the best of you: and being an absolute *Johannes fac totum*, is in his own conceit the only Shake-scene in a country.'

If the pun had not been enough to tell Shakespeare that he was the target of this tirade, the phrase pointedly set in italics would have made it plain: it is an angrily clever adaptation of a line from one of his early successes, *3 Henry VI*, in which the Duke of York rages at the appalling Queen Margaret with *O tiger's heart wrapped in a woman's hide*. Greene's allusive style obscures the plain sense of his complaint: he could be accusing Shakespeare of making his reputation by imitating his betters, or even by actually stealing their work; it is likelier that he is attacking Shakespeare as an 'upstart' simply because he is a relative newcomer among the rare wits of London, and, moreover, one with pretensions: he thinks, like Aesop's crow, that he can be taken for a nightingale even though, as a player, he is beautified only with the feathers the writers have lent him; and now he is setting up as a poet too, padding out his lines ('bombast' was the soft stuffing of clothes) to compete with the masters of blank verse; he thinks he can do everything, that he is a *Johannes fac totum* – a Jack-of-all-trades (as well as a Johnny-come-lately).

Clearly Shakespeare was becoming a success, and in an environment which must have seemed at first bewilderingly different from parochial Stratford with its pleasant elms. The City of London was a densely packed semi-circle, still bounded by the ancient walls with their seven gates. The westernmost of these,

Elizabethan London, from an engraving by Vissher

just north of the river at Blackfriars, was Ludgate, a prison as well as a gateway. In 1586, 'being sore decayed', it was 'clean taken down' and 'newly and beautifully' rebuilt,[29] and on its outer walls were images of the legendary King Lud and of Queen Elizabeth herself, so splendidly gilded that a novice arrived in the amazing city might think them to be truly made of gold.[30] From Ludgate the wall made its long curve past Newgate (also both gateway and prison), Aldersgate, Cripplegate, Moorgate, Bishopsgate and Aldgate, until it reached the river again, on the east side of the city, at the Tower. The river made the southern boundary; on it 3,000 or more watermen worked for hire in their little boats: it was a less troublesome way of crossing the city than by the crowded and dangerous streets.

The internal affairs of London were administered by the Lord Mayor and Aldermen, but some areas, including those known as 'Liberties' and parts of the suburbs, were outside their jurisdiction. The Puritanism of the London administration caused it to be unsympathetic to the theatre and sometimes at odds with the Queen and Council.

London had been spilling beyond its formal boundaries for some time. The main road to the north, after passing through the parish of St Helen's, where Shakespeare would lodge for a time, reached the wall and the old moat (now a stinking ditch) at Bishopsgate; it then led past Moor Fields, where laundresses spread out their washing, continued by the hospital for the mad, St Mary of Bethlehem, known as Bedlam, and, paved most of the way, went on to the suburb of Shoreditch and its playhouses. In the opposite direction the same road, under various names, cut southward through the city until it reached London Bridge, 'a work very rare' and in itself a busy thoroughfare: 'on both sides be houses built, so that it seemeth rather a continual street than a bridge.'[31] Across the bridge, on the further bank of the river was Southwark, eventually to be another of Shakespeare's addresses. It was dominated by the great church of St Saviour (once St Mary Overy), and nearby there were five prisons, St Thomas's Hospital (where six surgeons and one physician cared for 200 patients), two amphitheatres for animal shows and, newly built, the Rose Playhouse. The south bank was famous for its brothels, described disapprovingly by Aubrey as 'houses for the entertainment of lewd persons, in which were women prepared for all comers', and euphemistically by Shakespeare's Mistress Overdone as *our houses of resort in the suburbs*.[32] To the west of the city beyond Ludgate and across the Fleet River, a road (Fleet Street, becoming the Strand) connected London to the city of Westminster, running right through the grounds of the Queen's palace of Whitehall and on to Westminster Hall and the Abbey. Between the Strand and the river stood great houses, among them Somerset House, where Shakespeare and his fellows were later to attend on a Spanish envoy.

The whole of London, together with Westminster and the suburbs, covered an area perhaps three miles long and less than two miles wide, and into this space more than 150,000 people crowded. Numbers were increasing all the time, swollen by streams of incomers, and it was in vain that the authorities tried to control overcrowding by banning both the construction of new houses and the conversion of old ones into tenements. Inevitably London was a magnet for incomers like Shakespeare, looking for a place in the world, or like Field, bound apprentice to a London trade. There were foreign immigrants too, escaping bloody war in the Netherlands or fierce civil strife in France; after the turn of the century Shakespeare lodged with a Huguenot family. At any one time about 2,000 young men were riotously finishing their education at the Inns of Court and making of London something like a university town; many of them were up from the country, like Justice Silence's son William, who after his time at Oxford *must then to the Inns o'Court*.[33] Among the incomers the most worrying to the authorities were the huge numbers of vagrants driven by poverty, unemployment and dispossession: how best to deal with the poor was one of the preoccupying problems of the time. Some of the vagabonds were, of course, tricksters or petty criminals. The chronicler William Harrison counted 23 types of idle beggar, all with their own particular devices, like the palliards who applied corrosives or ratsbane to their flesh, 'thereby to raise pitiful and odious sores'. As a great city, London of course had a resourceful criminal underworld. While the vagabond, like Autolycus in *The Winter's Tale*, faced whipping, the pickpocket or cutpurse risked the gallows, since his crime was a felony, classed together (according to Harrison) with murder, rape, hunting by night with painted faces and visors, sodomy and buggery, stealing of hawk's eggs, sorcery, counterfeiting of coins and many other capital offences. It was a dangerous city, especially at night, in spite of the curfew rung out by the church bells, and even when, during the darker months, householders obeyed the Council's injunction and hung lanterns from their windows to guide benighted passers-by. It was uncommon, says Harrison, to see any Englishman 'to go without a dagger at the least at his back or by his side'.[34]

In this fast-moving world old certainties were shifting under the pressures of the actual – economic, demographic, technological, political. The life of the city was full of paradoxes; it was rigidly regulated but often disorderly, grandly ceremonial as well as disreputable; the Goldsmiths' Company enjoyed 'fair houses and shops' beautified with gilded images, while ditches and drains were neglected and 'dead dogs, cats, whelps or kitlings' were habitually thrown into the streets.[35] Naturally the fierce and complex energy of the city was reflected in the writing of the time. So was its cruelty. Modern students reading *Titus Andronicus* have been known to laugh uncomfortably at the famous stage direction *Enter a messenger with two heads and a hand*. Shakespeare's audiences would surely have found the moment shocking too, but the idea itself would not have seemed impossible, perhaps not even outlandish. Mutilation was a prescribed penalty; wholesale amputation was also known: for attacking the Queen's marriage plans the moralist John Stubbes was sentenced to the public severing of his right hand. Whenever Shakespeare walked from Southwark across the bridge he saw the parboiled heads of traitors impaled there – the Swiss visitor Thomas Platter counted more than 30 of them. Their quartered bodies were sometimes displayed at the city gates.

In London the growth of literacy was more rapid than elsewhere in the country; Shakespeare came to a city which was full of books. Traders often favoured particular streets or districts – the haberdashers kept shops on London Bridge, while grocers and apothecaries gave Bucklersbury a reputation for fragrance. The best place to find books was the churchyard of St Paul's, crowded with the premises of the booksellers, all with their identifying signs – the Green Dragon, the Gun, the Flower de Luce and Crown, the Mermaid. Commonly the same man was both publisher and bookseller; sometimes he was the printer too; but sometimes the functions were separated. Andrew Wise, for instance, published five of Shakespeare's plays, but most of these were printed for him by Valentine Simmes (an excellent craftsman whose colourful career led, after several prosecutions, to his being banned from work as a printer). Shakespeare's Sonnets were published by Thomas Thorpe and printed by George Elde – and some copies were sold by William Apsley, whose shop was at the sign of the Tiger's Head and later at the Parrot.

In spite of London's intellectual and creative buzz, it is very unlikely that Shakespeare set out with the intention of becoming a writer: it was not possible to make a living by the pen alone; a book once sold to the publisher became his property, and the writer could make no more money out of it. A pamphlet usually brought its author 40 shillings. For his great *Survey of London* John

Stow received £3 and 40 copies of the book; he died in poverty. Poetry was considered a civilised occupation for a nobleman like Sir Philip Sidney, for whom it was an art 'full of virtue-breeding delightfulness';[36] there was a whole 'crew of courtly makers, noble men and gentlemen of her Majesty's own servants' writing verses.[37] Lesser men had to find a livelihood – poets were often schoolmasters, secretaries, clergymen. But although the professional poet, as such, did not exist, there were, nevertheless, men for whom writing was their chief occupation and who had no other means of making a living. For them the only hope of avoiding poverty was to find a patron – they could be as fortunate as Ben Jonson, who received from the Earl of Pembroke an annual gift of £20 to buy books.

By royal warrant, the Stationers' Company monopolistically regulated the printing, publishing and selling of books. In theory (the practice was variable), any book intended for publication first had to receive a licence from a competent authority like the Bishop of London; this could involve censorship. The book then had to be registered (for a fee of sixpence) with the Stationers' Company. Since this entry in the Register established the book as the property of the publisher, it provided a sort of copyright protection.

However, there was one way for a fast and fluent writer to make a living by his pen alone: he could write plays. There had been important developments in the world of the players' companies. For some time, the yards of various inns had provided them with more or less permanent venues for their London performances: Tarlton of the Queen's Men played at the Bull in Bishopsgate Street, the Bel Savage on Ludgate Hill and the Bell in Gracechurch Street (and he went on to the Cross Keys, near the Bell, to see a performing horse 'of strange quality' called Morocco). But as early as 1567 a Bucklersbury grocer called John Brayne set about building what could have become a more permanent playhouse in Stepney. His venture petered out, but in 1576 he was persuaded to try again; the moving spirit in this new project was his brother-in-law, James Burbage, the carpenter turned actor who had been the leading signatory in the important 1572 petition of Leicester's Men to their patron. In April 1576 Burbage secured the necessary land on a 21-year lease from a certain Giles Allen, and by the next year his timber-built playhouse (though not quite complete) was open for business. It was in Shoreditch, it was called the Theatre, and it was the first true playhouse in London.

Within a very short time another playhouse, the Curtain, opened near the Theatre in Shoreditch. Another appeared, south of the river, in Newington, and in 1587 the great businessman Philip Henslowe (1555?–1616) opened the Rose in Southwark. Meanwhile a hall in what had once been the priory of Blackfriars was converted into an indoor theatre for public performances by the Children of the Chapel Royal. A chronicler of the period[38] was later to claim that 'within the space of threescore years' 17 stages and 'common playhouses' had been built in London and the suburbs (he included the inn-yards in his computation).

Shakespeare somehow found his way into the business of the playhouses. Samuel Johnson believed that 'he came to London a needy adventurer, and lived for a time by very mean employments ... His first expedient was to wait at the door of the playhouse, and hold the horses of those that had no servants'. It is rather likelier that he was working with a players' company, perhaps to begin with as a 'hired man', taking small parts and carrying out useful jobs; in good times a hired man could make ten shillings a week. Whatever the route, it is certain that Shakespeare became a player; and if this was a deliberate decision, it was an adventurous one for the young man brought up among burgesses, traders and farmers in Stratford. Church-going Bartholomew Hathaway could well have raised an eyebrow at his brother-in-law's choice of occupation – moralists were appalled at the new playhouses: 'Would to God,' wrote William Harrison, 'these common plays were exiled ... as seminaries of impiety, and their theatres pulled down, as no better than houses of bawdry. It is an evident token of a wicked time when players wax so rich that they can build such houses.'[39] The city authorities opposed the playhouses not only as ungodly, but also as nests of civil disorder, and breeding-grounds of infection in the plague seasons. Although the new houses were carefully situated outside the Lord Mayor's jurisdiction, they were harassed by restraints and threats of closure.

A hired man who could write plays was out of the ordinary, and useful too: the companies needed new plays. A house like the Rose could accommodate more than 2,000 spectators, and a company at full stretch presented six different plays each week; a new play was needed every fortnight or so. Plenty of jobbing writers – men like Shakespeare, educated and looking to earn a living – were available to work at turning out new plays, brushing up old ones, cobbling verse dramas out of legends, chronicles, classical sources and translated tales like the 'pleasant histories and excellent novels' collected in William Painter's *Palace of Pleasure* (1566, 1567, 1575). Many writers worked in collaboration with others, not unlike the teams of script-writers who feed the hunger of television companies. Thomas Dekker, for example, collaborated in the writing of 16 plays in one year.[40] In this business of collaborative writing and the patching-up of plays, it was not surprising that an author could suspect a younger rival of stealing his feathers.

The playhouses were not temples of high culture, but money-making concerns; the writers were not so much artists as suppliers,

The Children's Companies had their origin in performances of plays at humanist schools like St Paul's. Their success in giving what were effectively public performances was a curiosity of the period: during the first half of Elizabeth's reign they performed more often at court than the adults did. Their performances were clever, witty, sometimes scurrilous, and famous men enjoyed writing for them; Shakespeare mocked their popularity in *Hamlet*; Ben Jonson wrote a touching elegy on the death of a child-player, Salathiel (or Solomon) Pavy, 'the stage's jewel'.

and their plays were treated as commodities meeting a commercial need. A writer who was sole author of his play could sell it to a players' company for perhaps £6; it was likely to be his total gain, since the play then became the company's property. It was seldom in the interests of a company to release its playbooks, which were valuable assets as long as audiences kept on coming; so the majority of the plays written during this period were never published at all. Those plays that were printed appeared singly in the small, cheap editions known as quartos. Only half of Shakespeare's plays were published in this way during his lifetime, and the remainder first reached print seven years after his death, in the First Folio edition (1623) of his collected plays.[41] His name did not appear on a title-page until 1598.

However, while the writers of plays may have been seen as hacks, the plays were certainly not always hack work. In fact, the hungry market of the playhouses and the industry it generated brought about the creative explosion of Elizabethan and Jacobean drama, a development so rapid, profound and far-reaching that it has been described as a new mutation in English literature.[42] Of course, this extraordinary development did not spring fully-formed out of nothing. The drama of the 1580s was enriched by a confluence of earlier traditions: the Mystery Plays put on by the Guilds and Corporations of country towns; the allegorical Morality Plays (as much entertaining as moral) performed by the travelling companies; the learned classical plays and witty inter-ludes presented at court and in places of learning. A tradition of English stage comedy was already well-established.

The brightest spirits among the makers of plays during Shake-speare's early London years were the University Wits, the clique which included Robert Greene: their work played a crucial part in bringing about the transformation of Elizabethan drama. John Lyly (1554?–1606) wrote gracefully mannered prose comedies for the Blackfriars children; his aim was to evoke 'soft smiling, not

Christopher Marlowe (1564–93) in 1585

loud laughing'. Greene's *Friar Bacon and Friar Bungay* is more flamboyant, a jolly mixture of ringing verse and chatty prose. *The Old Wives' Tale* by George Peele (1557–96) is an even more enterprising mixture. The waspish controversialist Thomas Nashe (1567–1601) and romance writer Thomas Lodge (1558–1625) also helped in the turning-out of plays. Thomas Kyd (1558–94) was not strictly one of the Wits, since, like Shakespeare, he commanded only school learning; but he was closely (and, in the end, unhappily) associated with them. Though he was an unremarkable poet, he had a stronger sense of the theatre than any of the Wits. His masterpiece, *The Spanish Tragedy*, is extraordinary for its complex narrative, its exploitation of the theme of revenge, its elaborate cruelties, and its blending (in the famous last scene) of illusion and reality.

The most celebrated of the University Wits was Christopher Marlowe (1564–93): his two *Tamburlaine* plays were the sensational success of Shakespeare's early time in London. Unlike Kyd, Marlowe was not greatly skilled in organising a dramatic narrative; but, also unlike Kyd, he was a poet of genius. Blank verse had been seen as an appropriate form for the language of serious drama for two decades, but it could often be pedestrian or inflated with bombast – Nashe complained of the kind of uninspired writer who relied on 'the spacious volubility of a drumming decasyllabon'. Marlowe brought to blank verse a new sonority, the grandeur of his much imitated mighty line, which could in itself be limiting; Shakespeare added his own variety and flexibility.

By the time of Greene's attack Shakespeare had written several plays, perhaps partly in collaboration with other writers.[43] *The Two Gentlemen of Verona* reads as an amiable romance by a gifted poet aware of literary fashion and not yet very adventurous in exploring the possibilities of drama. The central matter of the story is conventional – ideal Friendship disrupted by ungovernable Love; it proceeds, without any serious raising of the emotional temperature, through treachery and loss, attempted rape, denunciation, sacrifice and forgiveness, and returns effortlessly to *one mutual happiness*. The verse is prettily patterned and sweet-toned, with moments of eloquence; it also sometimes rises to extravagance – the beloved Silvia is said to weep *a sea of melting pearl, which some call tears*. Already there are hints of that complexity of approach which led Shakespeare both to exploit and to mock the conventions of poetic love and its *wailful sonnets*. The strongest dramatic energy is in the relationship between the comic servant Launce and his dog Crab, *the sourest-natured dog that lives.* Although Launce shares a common lineage with Lyly's cheeky servants, the idiosyncratic prose Shakespeare has given him is a world away from their clever quips and witty fragments of Latin.

The virtuoso variety of another early comedy, *The Taming of the Shrew*,[44] suggests that Shakespeare was already experimenting consciously with different forms and effects. Like Peele's *Old Wives' Tale*, it has a 'frame', the Induction in which the drunken tinker Christopher Sly is gulled into losing touch with his Warwickshire reality.

Blank verse (unrhymed verse in ten-syllable lines, the stress falling on alternate syllables) was introduced into England by Henry Howard, Earl of Surrey (1517?–47), in his translation of parts of the *Aeneid*. This kind of deca-syllabic line, the iambic pentameter, quickly became the most popular medium for English verse. The first blank verse tragedy for the stage was *Gorboduc* (1562), by Thomas Norton (1532–84) and Thomas Sackville (1536–1608), who later became Baron Buckhurst, Earl of Dorset and Lord Treasurer of England.

While he and his companions sit *aloft*, players entertain him with the *pleasant comedy* of the Shrew. The opening of the play proper is very like *Two Gentlemen* in tone, but within 50 lines a wholly different sort of comedy takes over. Instead of the calm procession of duologues and soliloquies, it has a double plot and a rush of crowded episodes, delivered with exhilarating changes of style: quick-fire repartee, sardonic asides, joyously discursive prose, lyric love-poetry, irresistible rhyming verse – as when Petruchio promises brave revelling:

> *With silken coats, and caps, and golden rings,*
> *With ruffs, and cuffs, and farthingales, and things …*

The climax of the play is Kate's speech of submission, a

celebration of the hierarchical order of things in which a wife's duty is *to serve, love, and obey* her *lord*, her *king*, her *governor*. This manifesto takes 44 lines of grandly measured blank verse, with occasional clinching rhymes; and after it Petruchio at once returns to idiomatic reality: *Why, there's a wench! Come on, and kiss me, Kate.*

Shakespeare's first tragedy, *Titus Andronicus*, is a revenge play, influenced by Kyd's *Spanish Tragedy*, and even more sensationally cruel.[45] However, it is not merely a gory tale: Shakespeare was trying his skill at an academic play, a tragedy after Roman models, and the agonies of rape, mutilation and murder are presented in stately verse that blurs the edges of reality, sometimes with extraordinary elegance:

Alas, a crimson river of warm blood,
Like to a bubbling fountain stirred with wind,
Doth rise and fall between thy rosed lips,
Coming and going with thy honey breath.
But sure some Tereus hath deflowered thee.

Shakespeare draws several times on the cruel myth of the rape of Philomel by King Tereus, which he found in Ovid's *Metamorphoses*. The poet Ted Hughes, who himself translated parts of the *Metamorphoses*, held that Shakespeare shared with Ovid a taste for the extreme, the tortured, the grotesque; and he thought *Titus* in a sense Shakespeare's most Ovidian work.[46] The play is allowed some wicked comedy in the figure of the arch-villain, Aaron the Moor, a Machiavel who sneers at the *thing ... called conscience* and, while he murders, mocks his victim: *'Wheak, wheak' – so cries a pig prepared to the spit.* There is a telling moment when he saves his new-born bastard child from death, and rails on the Nurse who calls the black baby loathsome: *Zounds, ye whore, is black so base a hue?* And for the baby itself he even shows a rough affection:

Look how the black slave smiles upon the father,
As who should say 'Old lad, I am thine own.'

For a moment, perhaps, Shakespeare is stepping beyond stereotype.

It seems to have been the success of Shakespeare's early histories, the three *Henry VI* plays,[47] that most nettled Greene – and no wonder: they were certainly the most remarkable history plays that had yet been written. It is possible that the majestic achievement of Marlowe's great tragical-historical two-parter *Tamburlaine* moved Shakespeare to try for his own epic drama, and that he turned to English, rather than exotic, history in response to the mood of exultant Englishness which followed the defeat of the Spanish Armada. He was by no means the first or the only writer of plays to forage in English history, and there was plenty of available material; Holinshed's *Chronicles*, newly republished, provided a favourite goldmine.[48] However, Shakespeare's sense of nationhood is not simple chauvinism of the usual kind, as expressed in the last line of Greene's *Friar Bacon*: 'Thus glories England over all the west.' The ambivalence that marked all his histories was there from the beginning.

Surprisingly, and ambitiously, Shakespeare chose to dramatise the long and fearsomely confused period of dynastic struggle between the death of Henry V (*too famous to live long*) and the coming of the Tudor golden age. In this reading of history England's greatness is darkened by division and disorder; the story dwells on guilt and retribution, or expiation. There is some straightforward tub-thumping against *the subtle-witted French*, but the English do not come gloriously out of the war against them. The brave Talbot is a patriot, but he is *entrapped* by the *fraud of England, not the force of France*. He and his equally dauntless son are victims of the *ancient bickerings* of the English nobility – and they die as proper stage heroes in a long outburst of resolutely rhyming verse. For the bickerings Shakespeare developed a more remarkable style, rhetoric of extraordinary ferocity, and they take up most of the narrative.

His vision of a disordered realm is a large one: it includes the people, usually presented as capricious and gullible:

> *The commons, like an angry hive of bees*
> *That want their leader, scatter up and down*
> *And care not who they sting ...*

They are also capable of suffering, and the disorder brings distress. In one sad incident a simple trickster and his wife are caught and sentenced to a whipping, and while the noblemen exchange jokes, the woman pleads *Alas, sir, we did it for pure need.* The longest irruption of the commons into the main action is Jack Cade's rebellion, perhaps the most innovative episode in the cycle, and not wholly comic. Cade meets his end, claiming *Famine and no other hath slain me*, in the garden of a Kentish squire, Alexander Iden; Cade's vigorous prose (*I'll make thee eat iron like an ostrich and swallow my sword like a great pin*) is set against Iden's sober and conventional verse with exactly calculated contrast. In one of the most telling scenes the collapse of order is conveyed with a kind of solemn ritual which draws on the emblematic method of an earlier dramatic tradition: at a crisis point of the *fell war*, the gentle king sits on the ground, alone, exhaustedly longing for a simple life and *a quiet grave*, and, while he reflects, *Enter a Son that hath kill'd his Father, at one door: and a Father that hath kill'd his Son at another door*; each mourner bears a body in his arms; to their antiphonal grief the king adds his own lamentation:

> *O piteous spectacle! O bloody times!*
> *Whiles lions war and battle for their dens,*
> *Poor harmless lambs abide their enmity.*

The third play closes with drums and trumpets as the new king, Edward IV, calls for *stately triumphs, mirthful comic shows* to celebrate his hope of *lasting joy*. But Shakespeare clearly did not intend the violent story to end there. He completed his first cycle of histories with *Richard III*,[49] his most ambitious and assured play yet, and one of the longest he ever wrote, a huge melodrama held together by the tremendous central character. Though the gleeful villain was a traditional stage figure, Shakespeare carries Richard beyond the stereotypical by the inventive brilliance of the language in which this *elvish-marked, abortive, rooting hog*, this *foul bunch-backed toad*, is presented and presents himself. Underlying the dramatic energy of the diction is Shakespeare's most skilful and extensive use of the arts of rhetoric. There is, of course, much word-play, often of a kind more subtle than York's simple aural pun earlier in the cycle: *for Suffolk's duke, may he be suffocate*. It is often witty (the ironist Richard likes to *moralise two meanings in one word*) and can also be piercingly effective, as in the duel of words between Richard and the widowed Queen, who knows he has brought about the murder in the Tower of her two little sons; when he snaps at her with *Your reasons are too shallow and too quick*, she at once caps his line:

> *O no, my reasons are too deep and dead –*
> *Too deep and dead, poor infants, in their graves.*[50]

In *Richard III* the whole history cycle is drawn together by the obsessive recalling of past hatreds and griefs, the bitterness intensely conveyed by the formally shaped language. As he moves towards *his piteous and unpitied end*, Richard briefly imagines his own sins *crying all, 'Guilty, guilty!'*, but there is no comforting repentance. At the end of the play, victorious Richmond (now the first Tudor king) again recalls the agony of the disordered realm:

England hath long been mad, and scarred herself;
The brother blindly shed the brother's blood;
The father rashly slaughtered his own son;
The son, compelled, been butcher to the sire ...

With an already assured sense of the dramatic, Shakespeare avoids easy triumphalism and closes the cycle, now a tetralogy, with a quiet prayer for peace.

Variable Passions 1592–4

The publication of *Greene's Groatsworth* seems to have created a minor storm, or what Nashe called 'a coil of pamphleting'. Within a few weeks its editor, Henry Chettle, thought it proper, or prudent, to publish a disclaimer and an apology. In a pamphlet of his own, *Kind-Heart's Dream*, he protested that he had had no part in the writing and that 'it was all Greene's, not mine nor Master Nashe's, as some unjustly have affirmed' (in fact Nashe had already published his own indignant rejection of Greene's 'scald trivial lying pamphlet'). Chettle claimed that he had merely acted as copyist, needed because 'it was ill written, as sometime Greene's hand was none of the best'. More significant than this disclaimer is Chettle's apology. He regrets the attack on Shakespeare, 'as if the original fault had been my fault, because myself have seen his demeanour no less civil, than he excellent in the quality he professes' – his profession of acting; moreover, Chettle continues, some important people ('divers of worship') have testified to Shakespeare's uprightness of dealing, his honour and the polished ('facetious') grace of his writing.[51] It is not known who these important people were, but their support of the young Shakespeare seems to have impressed Chettle. At any rate Shakespeare was never attacked in that way again, nor did he ever quarrel with other writers – a rarity in a polemical age.

With audiences his plays were already popular. According to Nashe, 'brave Talbot' on the stage drew 'the tears of ten thousand spectators …'.[52] But though the plays were evidently being performed, and successfully too, it is not clear which companies Shakespeare worked with, or wrote for, during these early years. Henslowe recorded healthily profitable performances by Lord Strange's Men of a play which was probably *Henry VI*, and the title-page of the first printed edition of *Titus* indicates that it was played (and presumably owned) by three different companies. However, by the autumn of 1592 it must have seemed far from certain that any company at all was in a position to offer Shakespeare a safe future in the public playhouse. Trouble began in June of that year with 'a great disorder and tumult' in Southwark. The Lord Mayor, attending 'with all speed', found that the disturbance was caused by 'certain servants of the feltmakers' together with 'a great number of loose and masterless men apt for such purposes'. A fellow apprentice had been imprisoned in the Marshalsea, and they intended to rescue him, gathering there 'by occasion and pretence of their meeting at a play'.[53] It was reason enough to take action. On the Lord Mayor's complaint the Privy Council closed the playhouses. It is possible that this damaging restraint would have been lifted before long, but in fact it became irrelevant: the playhouses – and London in general – were attacked by a more dangerous enemy.

The plague seemed to have retreated from the city – it had been almost wholly absent for nine years. But in August 1592 it was back, and it very soon became clear that this was to be an unusually long-lasting and ferocious visitation. The horror continued for nearly two years. Londoners carried pomanders and burned bunches of rue to keep the danger away, or placed an onion on the ground to absorb the infection. Fires were lit outside the houses. Apprentices were forbidden to indulge in 'the outrageous play at football' in the streets for fear of spreading the disease. Profit from the capture of the Portuguese galleon *Madre de Dios* was earmarked for building a plague hospital (but it was still unfinished in 1603). Any house thought to be infected was boarded up and its door marked with the cross of St Antony and the words LORD HAVE MERCY ON US; 'sober ancient women' were detailed to bring necessaries to the wretched people, sick or healthy, imprisoned within.[54] In *Christ's Tears over Jerusalem* Nashe agonised over this 'sin-procured scourge', and prayed for the Lord's comfort: 'with so many funerals are we oppressed that we have no leisure to weep for our sins for howling for our sons and daughters. O hear the voice of our howling, withdraw thy hand from us …'

Puritans and preachers knew where the blame lay: years earlier the city authorities had warned that 'to play in plaguetime is to increase the plague by infection: to play out of plaguetime is to draw the plague by offending God upon occasion of such plays'.[55] The playhouses, which had already been restrained in June 1592, remained closed, with the exception of a few winter weeks, until the early summer of 1594. The players' companies took to the road, with reduced numbers, for months at a time, forsaking 'the stately and our more than Roman city stages, to travel upon the hard hoof from village to village for cheese and buttermilk'.[56] The actor Edward Alleyn was writing anxiously to his wife in London, begging for news, warning her to keep good store of rue in the house, reminding her to turn the parsley bed over to spinach. It is not impossible that Shakespeare was among the travellers. Strange's Men were given a special licence to play anywhere in the kingdom not less than seven miles outside London, and named in the licence were several players who were to become – perhaps already were – Shakespeare's friends. His name, however, is not on the list, and it is pleasant to imagine that he might have spent some of this troubled time in Stratford: his children were growing, and his brother Edmund, approaching his teens, was perhaps already thinking of becoming a player. John Shakespeare, in trouble, accused of not attending church 'for fear of process for debt', might perhaps have welcomed his son's help. In 1594 the Stratford Schoolmaster Alexander Aspinall (John Cottam's successor) married the widow of a Shakespeare family friend; as a courtship present Aspinall gave the lady a pair of gloves, together with a tiny poem:

'The gift is small;
The will is all:
Alexander Aspinall.'

A beguiling tradition holds that John Shakespeare made the gloves and his son wrote the poem. Unfortunately, however, there is no evidence at all either that Shakespeare was in Stratford at this time, or that he was touring, and it is equally possible that he spent the plague years, busy writing, in stricken London.

Since nobody could know how long the closure of the playhouses would last, it would be necessary for Shakespeare to consider a change of direction: as a poet now working outside the paying business of the theatre he must hope to find a patron. Henry Wriothesley, Earl of Southampton (1573–1624) was 19 years old, a youthful grandee and already much admired. This ornamental young man seems to have had a civilised regard for learning (he was later to give generously to the Bodleian Library, and books from his own library went to his old college, St John's, Cambridge) and he was known to delight in plays. Inevitably writers saw him as a possible patron. The clever John Florio (1545–1625) was already in his entourage. In fact (this is to anticipate) Southampton turned out not to be a very useful patron. Volatile and self-willed, he often found himself in serious trouble at court; he involved himself deeply in faction, following the star of his hero, the Earl of Essex; his debts grew. Not surprisingly, he was not always in a position to

Shakespeare's patron Henry Wriothesley, Earl of Southampton
(1573–1624)

be generous: it is interesting that Nashe, after including with *The Unfortunate Traveller* (1594) a flattering dedication promising to canonise the young lord's name to posterity, withdrew it from the second edition. In the end, relatively few books were dedicated to Southampton; two of Shakespeare's, however, were among them.

The first was his narrative poem *Venus and Adonis*. In the elegant prefatory letter addressed to Southampton Shakespeare hopes that 'the first heir of my invention' will not disappoint 'so noble a godfather'; if it pleases, the poet will 'take advantage of all idle hours' to work on 'some graver labour' for his patron. The implication seems to be that, light as it is, this poem is his first real creation, and not related to the ephemeral commerce of the playhouse; on the title page is an epigraph from Ovid which indicates that the poet intends to rise above the cheapjack arts which amaze the common herd. Shakespeare took his poem to be printed by his Stratford acquaintance Richard Field, who was producing fine books (he had just printed a translation of Ariosto by the Queen's godson, Sir John Harington), and it was sold at the sign of the White Greyhound by the bookseller John Harrison, who later bought the copyright.

Venus and Adonis is a gorgeous expansion of a tale from the *Metamorphoses*: the goddess Venus, in love with a beautiful youth, tries to seduce him, but he refuses to yield – he prefers to go hunting. It is a poem in the height of fashion, erotic and intelligent; it contains playful homilies on the obligations of beauty and the difference between love and lust; there are broadly comic moments and bouts of witty dialogue, she pleading, he tetchy. The most celebrated passages are those in which the *variable passions* are reflected in the world outside the protagonists, like the scene in which a tethered stallion is spied by a flirting mare and, breaking his rein, *to her straight goes he*. Even the boar's fatal attack on Adonis is presented as an act of tender sexuality:

> *'Tis true, 'tis true, thus was Adonis slain:*
> *He ran upon the boar with his sharp spear,*

Who did not whet his teeth at him again,
But by a kiss thought to persuade him there,
And, nuzzling in his flank, the loving swine
Sheathed unaware the tusk in his soft groin.

Venus closes the poem with a vengeful prophecy: since her *rose-cheeked Adonis* is dead, she decrees that *sorrow on love hereafter shall attend*; and in her chariot drawn by silver doves she drives away through the empty skies to Paphos, where she will remain hidden forever.

There is no way of knowing whether Shakespeare wrote his poem and its dedication speculatively, hoping to catch the eye of a patron, or whether he had already been noticed by Southampton. The poem may have been written with a purpose. Southampton was in a difficult situation: since becoming fatherless at an early age he had been the ward of William Cecil, Lord Burghley (1520–98), Elizabeth's powerful Lord Treasurer; Burghley was determined that his granddaughter, Elizabeth Vere, should become the wife of his young ward. Southampton refused, on the grounds that he did not wish to marry at all, and this refusal made him liable to a crippling fine – it was said to be £5,000. Inevitably there was pressure on the Earl to change his mind, and it is possible that Shakespeare's tale of a handsome youth resisting the approach of love was part of a campaign; he may have been commissioned to write it, perhaps by the Earl's mother and perhaps through an intermediary like Florio. But if so, the poem was not very cleverly aimed: the Queen of Love is sometimes more absurd than seductive, red and sweating with desire – and hefty too: she imprisons the sulky boy under one arm while she tethers his horse to a tree. It is just as likely that Shakespeare knew of Southampton's predicament and was artfully expressing sympathy.

The gift cannot have displeased the patron, since Shakespeare at once turned to the *graver labour* he had promised. His second narrative poem, *The Rape of Lucrece*, again printed by Richard

Field, appeared in 1594. Though its dedication to Southampton is expressed with proper humility, some readers have sensed in it a tone of more personal warmth: *The love I dedicate to your lordship is without end ... What I have done is yours; what I have to do is yours, being part in all I have, devoted yours.* Both Shakespeare's narrative poems deal with the importunacy of desire, but in *Lucrece* the effect is of high seriousness. The first part of the poem is intensely dramatic: the shame which tortures *lust-breathed Tarquin* as he steals towards the chamber of Lucrece is conveyed in nightmare images – a grating door, shrieks of *night-wandering weasels*, his torch-smoke blowing back in his face, the hidden needle that pricks him as he touches her glove. His crime destroys them both, and afterwards he creeps away *like a thievish dog*. The whole of the rest of the poem, more than 1,000 lines of it, is given to her despair, and here it achieves the promised gravity. Her suicide is narrated in a solemn pattern of chiasmus and antithesis:

Both the young people eventually found other partners. Elizabeth Vere (whose father had been that Earl of Oxford of whom Aubrey tells his funniest story) married the younger brother of Ferdinando, Lord Strange, and so in time became Countess of Derby. Southampton went on to have an affair with Elizabeth Vernon, cousin of the Earl of Essex and a Maid of Honour to the Queen. She became pregnant, and they married secretly, without royal consent, for which breach of protocol Southampton was disgraced and imprisoned.

> *Even here she sheathed in her harmless breast*
> *A harmful knife, that thence her soul unsheathed ...*

It is to be hoped that Southampton approved of the poems – there is no record of his response. Nicholas Rowe, more than a century later, reported that Southampton 'at one time' gave Shakespeare £1,000, a gift, he added sourly, almost equal to the generosity his own age showed to French dancers and Italian eunuchs.

The story has been widely dismissed as incredible; Southampton's finances were not stable, and such a gift (it would have been by far the greatest ever bestowed by a patron on a poet) would surely have attracted some comment. Shakespeare never again dedicated a book to a patron. Certainly both poems were much admired by discriminating readers. That this admiration faltered in later centuries – Hazlitt described them as being 'like a couple of ice-houses ... as hard, as glittering, and as cold'[57] – is partly due to the revolt of the Romantic imagination against conscious artifice. But Shakespeare himself never forsook the artifices of rhetoric, although he deployed them with increasing originality; they underpin the language of his mature plays, the incoherence of Lear no less than the wit of Falstaff. The narrative poems built his reputation as a serious poet, and both went into several editions during his lifetime. A fellow-poet celebrated the 'honey-flowing vein' of Shakespeare,

'Whose *Venus*, and whose *Lucrece* (sweet and chaste)
Thy name in fame's immortal book have placed .'[58]

Some at least of Shakespeare's 154 Sonnets were written during the 1590s: the publication in 1591 of Sidney's *Astrophil and Stella* set off a fashion for sonnet-sequences which lasted for a decade or so. Although Shakespeare's Sonnets were not published until later,[59] they were known in manuscript by 1598, when a writer referred to Shakespeare's 'sugared sonnets among his private friends'.[60] They are not narrative poems in the usual sense, but they hint at an elusive story: a passionate relationship seems to develop into a bisexual triangle, an emotional confusion which is announced with untypical directness in Sonnet 144:

Two loves I have, of comfort and despair ...
The better angel is a man right fair,
The worser spirit a woman coloured ill.

The first 126 poems spring from the Poet's devotion to a young man, *the master-mistress of my passion*, and the remaining 28 from his intense and difficult affair with a woman, a Dark Lady whose *eyes are raven-black*. It seems that neither of these loves is untroubled.

His relationship with the Youth involves, besides idealised and self-denying devotion, mistrust, jealousy, neglect and betrayal; the liaison with the Dark Lady drives the Poet through lust and self-hatred to the point where he is *frantic mad* (Sonnet 147); the last two poems of the sequence even hint at a venereal infection with which the Poet is *distempered*.

Although the term 'Sonnet' was sometimes used to indicate any kind of short poem, it also specifically referred to a poem of 14 decasyllabic lines, of the kind brought to England from Italy by Sir Thomas Wyatt (1503–42). Sonnets took different forms: the English (or Shakespearean) Sonnet was composed of three quatrains (each with alternately rhyming lines), followed by a rhyming couplet.

The intimate and allusive tone of the Sonnets has led many readers to regard them as autobiographical, perhaps literally so, or perhaps as possibly unconscious revelations of Shakespeare's inner life. His own contemporaries apparently did not read them in that way; nor did his early biographers. The belief that the Shakespeare of the Sonnets was writing about his own experiences and passions had to wait for 200 years, and for the Romantic imagination to seize on them; but now this belief is widely (not universally) held. Various originals have been suggested for the persons of the story. The possible Dark Ladies have included the remarkable Emilia Lanier, the Lord Chamberlain's mistress – she was of Italian descent; eventually she became a poet in her own right. The Rival Poet who competes for the attention of the Fair Youth could have been George Chapman. The mysterious 'Mr W H' to whom the first published edition was dedicated may not be the Youth – he was perhaps Southampton's step-father, Sir William Harvey, who could have provided the publisher with the manuscript. Favourites for the Fair Youth include Southampton, of course; another is William Herbert, Earl of Pembroke (1580–1630) – if he was the Youth, the Sonnets would probably not have been written before the late 1590s. Both these young aristocrats caused concern by their reluctance to marry, and the first 17 Sonnets, like *Venus and Adonis*, can be seen as elegant instruments of persuasion: though marriage itself is hardly mentioned, the Youth is urged to perpetuate his beauty by begetting children.

One of the first exponents of the Romantic approach was August Wilhelm von Schlegel (1767–1845), the German translator of Shakespeare. In his 1808 lectures *On Dramatic Art and Literature* he condemned all earlier critics for failing to see that the Sonnets 'describe quite obviously real situations and moods of the poet' and 'contain remarkable confessions of his youthful errors '.[61]

The biographical approach to the Sonnets can seem to promise exciting revelations, 'the whole terrible, sinful, magical story of Shakespeare's passion'.[62] Even among more sober readers, it inevitably sets off speculation, not least about the Poet's feelings for the Youth whose androgynous beauty recalls both Adonis and Helen of Troy (Sonnet 53). Ideal friendship between men was a favourite subject of Renaissance writing, and it sometimes involved an extravagance of expression, and apparently of feeling, that seems curious today; Shakespeare's gentlemen of Verona address each other in their first scene as *my loving Proteus* and *sweet Valentine*. While the Poet's desire for the Dark Lady is unambiguously physical, his love of the Youth (despite the frequent celebration of his beauty) does indeed seem to take a more idealised form. It was not unknown for an Elizabethan poet to use the language of explicit and physical homosexual passion, as for instance in the sonnets of Richard Barnfield:

'Sometimes I wish that I his pillow were,
So I might steal a kiss, and yet not seen,

> So I might gaze upon his sleeping eyne,
> Although I did it with a panting fear ...'[63]

But there is nothing like this in the Sonnets, no unambiguous indication that the Poet's passion is physical, let alone sinful or terrible.

On the other hand, it is undeniable that conventional male friendship can be the sublimation, or even the deliberate masking, of a more fleshly affection – Corydon masquerading as Damon. Moreover it is impossible to ignore the intensely personal feeling of the Sonnets. The happy heterosexual lovers who now quote *Shall I compare thee to a summer's day?* (Sonnet 18) would perhaps be surprised to discover that this ecstatic poem is addressed to a friend, and a male friend at that – it is so obviously a love poem. The interesting, and unanswerable, question is not whether the love is homosexual (it surely is, in some sense), but whether it is fictional or autobiographical.

Within the close limits of his sonnet form Shakespeare varies the structure of his poems with astonishing virtuosity. The diction too is extraordinarily varied (a pressing reason to believe that the Sonnets were written over a period of years). The language is often complex, so tightly packed as to be puzzling – in Sonnet 112, for instance:

> *None else to me, nor I to none alive,*
> *That my steeled sense or changes, right or wrong.*

Words are pressed into unfamiliar forms and uses – the Poet surfeits by *gluttoning*; he fears Time's *millioned accidents*; he begs the Youth to *o'er-green my bad*; he knows no art but *mutual render, only me for thee*. Shakespeare of course revels in artifices of all kinds, even though in Sonnet 82 he has the Poet affect to despise the *strained touches* of rhetoric and prefer *true plain words*. In the greater sonnets the artifices perfectly match the ideas: the elaborate play of sense and sound in the wonderful Sonnet 43 (*When most I wink*) conveys the deceptiveness of a dream. The imagery can be surprising, or elaborate, as when summer's sweetness is presented as a rare essence kept frozen in winter, *a liquid prisoner pent in walls of glass*. Familiar imagery sometimes takes on new life: a favourite Elizabethan commonplace pictured the world as a stage, observed by Heaven or the gods; in Sonnet 15 this metaphorical audience takes on a specially mysterious quality:

> ... *this huge stage presenteth naught but shows*
> *Whereon the stars in secret influence comment.*

One of the strong impressions left by a reading of the Sonnets is of the writer's preoccupation with Time: a sense of its *thievish progress to eternity* is often the counterpoint to the passions of the poems, and embodied in image after image – the *cruel knife* and the *fell hand*, the *surly sullen bell*, the transience of summer, the fire dying *on the ashes of his youth*, desert wastes and *mouthed graves*, the delving of *parallels in beauty's brow*. The Poet issues his challenges (*do thy worst, old Time*), and sets up defences against oblivion: the begetting of children; the immortalising power of verse, which is more lasting than brass; love itself, which is *not Time's fool*. But the last lines addressed to the Youth gently remind him that after all Nature must pay her debt to Time: death is inevitable. In the context of this preoccupation, one of the most unexpected poems is Sonnet 146, which would not seem out of place among the *Holy Sonnets* of John Donne. It is a poem of spiritual conflict, the familiar dispute between the soul, *the centre of my sinful earth,* and the body which is food for worms. The Poet addresses his own soul:

> *So shalt thou feed on death, that feeds on men,*
> *And death once dead, there's no more dying then.*

Also somewhat in the manner of Donne is Shakespeare's most famous short poem, now known as *The Phoenix and the Turtle* – it was originally published without a title.[64] This mysterious poem has inevitably attracted a number of allegorical interpretations, but the surface symbolism is explicit enough: the Phoenix and the Turtle-dove are Love and Constancy, and they are dead: the poem is a formal lament. But it is also appropriately included among Shakespeare's poems of love, a magnificent celebration of the *mutual flame* by which two souls become one even while they remain *two distincts* – Reason itself cries out *How true a twain Seemeth this concordant one!*.

The Poet of the Sonnets sometimes expresses dissatisfaction with his way of life:

> ... *I have gone here and there*
> *And made myself a motley to the view* ...

Fortune has condemned him to seek his livelihood in a basely public way. This may, of course, be Shakespeare's own voice speaking through his Poet – the sentiment is an extension of the idea in the epigraph to *Venus and Adonis*, which consigned cheap work to the vulgar multitude; but this fastidiousness, if it really is Shakespeare's own, certainly did not keep him from writing plays which would ultimately delight that same multitude when the playhouses resumed business. *The Comedy of Errors* may well date from this period;[65] its first recorded performance was on 28 December, Holy Innocents' Day, 1594, as part of the Christmas celebrations at Gray's Inn (where Southampton had once been among the young gentlemen finishing their education). It was, not unexpectedly, a rowdy occasion, marked by 'throngs and tumults, crowds and outrages', and after some 'dancing and revelling with gentlewomen ... a Comedy of Errors (like to Plautus his *Menechmus*) was played by the players. So that night was begun, and continued to the end, in nothing but confusion and errors; whereupon, it was ever afterwards called, *The Night of Errors*.[66]

The play was an apt choice for private performance among the budding lawyers – short, clever, very funny and impeccably modelled on Roman comedy. Shakespeare's source was one of the most popular of these Roman plays, Plautus's *Menaechmi*, which tells the story of a twin searching for his long-lost brother. Shakespeare boldly multiplied the farcical permutations by adding a second pair of parted twins, servants to the first pair; he also allowed himself some serious touches by adding a baffled and jealous wife, some pretty love-talk and a grieving father. Both time and location are classically controlled and specific. After a prologue scene, the story itself begins at dinner-time:

> *The capon burns, the pig falls from the spit.*
> *The clock hath strucken twelve upon the bell ...*

And the headless confusion continues by way of several interventions from the clock until *the dial point's at five*. The action takes place in the streets of Ephesus (famous for its *dark-working sorcerers* – which exist only in the travellers' minds) in front of three 'houses', represented perhaps by doorways giving on to the acting area, or by sections of an arcade in the Italian manner. Two are clearly identified; the third, at first mysterious, turns out to be *some Priory*; and from this sacred place emerges the Abbess whose stately intervention unravels all the errors. The shaping of this improbable story involves a formula which Shakespeare found useful more than once: the characters are lost in a strange world, dream or nightmare, where they *wander in illusions*; in this wandering even identity is lost, and not found again until the end of the story. It is with this uncertainty that the Syracusan twin begins his search:

I to the world am like a drop of water
That in the ocean seeks another drop,
Who, falling there to find his fellow forth,
Unseen, inquisitive, confounds himself.

Another play, *Love's Labour's Lost*,[67] may belong to the period of the poems of love; there are verbal correspondences, and the fragile plot glances lightly at some of the same preoccupations. The King of Navarre and his courtiers resolve to defeat *cormorant devouring time* by abstinence and study; the Princess of France arrives with a retinue of *mocking wenches* (including a *whitely wanton* with pitch-black eyes); the gentlemen yield to the *almighty dreadful little might* of Cupid. Within this simple narrative almost nothing happens. Pleasantly strolling about, there are folk from some Firbankian country community, the parson, the schoolmaster, the constable, and a braggart soldier, the kind of prickly fellow who, wrote Coleridge, 'even in my time was not extinct in the cheaper inns of North Wales'.[68] The characters fleet the time carelessly with talk, flirtation, writing verses, a half-hour nap in *the cool shade of a sycamore*, fancy dress and a villagers' entertainment. But at the very last moment *the scene begins to cloud*: a messenger brings the news that the Princess's father has died. When reality invades the idyll, love simply has to wait; it is not the time *to make a world-without-end bargain*. The unresolved ending is one of Shakespeare's most remarkable inventions:

Our wooing doth not end like an old play.
Jack hath not Jill ...

It may well be that *Love's Labour's Lost* was intended, at first, for private performance; certainly the allusiveness of the wit suggests the in-jokes of a coterie. Some of the characters have been seen as lightly mocking portraits: the impudent page Moth, for instance, may be Nashe, with his butt Gabriel Harvey disguised as Holofernes, and John Florio as Armado. But the satire, if there is any, is hurtless. Although the play ridicules fashionable quirks and extravagances of language, there is more enjoyment than mockery in Shakespeare's treatment: it is his most exuberantly wordy play, a *great feast of languages*, in which a character can prefer *festinately* to 'hastily', or speak of *the posteriors of this day, which the rude multitude call the afternoon*. The whole play is perfumed with the *sweet smoke of rhetoric*; even when the courtier Berowne promises to give up all artificiality of expression, he does so with an elegant metaphor, forswearing *taffeta phrases, silken terms precise* in favour of *russet yeas, and honest kersey noes* (kersey was a rough woollen cloth). An actor in this play has to get his tongue round Shakespeare's most amazing word: *honorificabilitudinitatibus*. Shakespeare did not invent it, but he must have been delighted to find it. An unknown Elizabethan once wrote that he found 'greater grace and majesty in longer words, so they be current English. Monosyllables are good to make up a gobbling and huddling verse'.[69] Shakespeare may well have agreed – even when the word he was enjoying could scarcely be called current, or indeed English.

Perhaps it is not surprising that this curious, leisurely, allusive play fell into neglect in later times – there is no record of a performance between the closing of the theatres in 1642 and the beginning of Queen Victoria's reign. When it was at last revived, at Covent Garden in 1839, it was in a diluted version, with many cuts.[70] However, it was admired in Shakespeare's own time, even when the brightness of the in-jokes must have worn off. At the beginning of the next reign, the courtier Sir Walter Cope, casting about for an entertainment to please James I's Queen, Anne of Denmark, had been hunting all morning for 'players, jugglers and such kind of creatures … leaving notes for them to seek me'. Eventually word came that 'there is no new play that the Queen hath not seen, but they have revived an old one called *Love's Labour's*

Lost, which for wit and mirth … will please her exceedingly. And this is appointed to be played tomorrow night at my Lord of Southampton's'.[71]

Fellowship in a cry of players 1594–6

No wonder the 'Night of Errors' at Gray's Inn was boisterous: it was the Christmas season in a liberated city. By the early summer of 1594 it was clear that the plague had retreated, the players were in business again, and a new phase was beginning in the story of the London theatre and of Shakespeare's career. The closure had brought changes. During the long months of travelling, players' companies splintered and merged, 'broke' altogether, or withdrew from London and became provincial troupes. Actors migrated from one troupe to another. Out of the shuffling emerged the two great companies that were to dominate the London playhouses for more than a decade. Both had powerful patrons. The Admiral's Men enjoyed the protection of one of the Queen's kinsmen, Lord Howard of Effingham (1536–1624); he had been Lord High Admiral since 1585 – his prudence (together with God's winds and the nippy English ships) was crucial in the defeat of the Armada. One of his Company's strongest assets was the heroic actor Edward Alleyn (1566–1626), who was much admired as Marlowe's Tamburlaine. The Company finances were managed by Philip Henslowe, and when in 1592 Alleyn married Henslowe's step-daughter, Joan, the Company of the Admiral's Men became in effect a family firm, based at the Rose.

The patron of the other acting company, the Chamberlain's Men, was the Admiral's father-in-law, Henry Carey, Lord Hunsdon (1524–96). He too was kinsman to the Queen, certainly her cousin and probably her half-brother too (his mother was Anne Boleyn's sister and Henry VIII was said to have looked amorously on both ladies). The Company could scarcely have found a more useful patron than the irascible Lord Hunsdon: as Lord Chamberlain he had authority over the Revels Office, which organised plays and entertainments at court. It was a serious task: under the Master of the Revels, Edmund Tilney (1535?–1610), the Office investigated and controlled every detail. Before presentation, plays had first to be 'recited' to Tilney or his deputy; the players, with all their paraphernalia, had to trudge along to the Revels Office in Clerkenwell; it was in part of the building which had once been the Hospital of St John of Jerusalem, and the suite of rooms included a great chamber convenient for rehearsal and performance. The authority of the Master of the Revels was gradually extended until he was responsible for controlling and licensing all plays and playhouses (in return for appropriate fees, naturally). His licence often involved censorship, but it was also, to some degree, a protection for the companies against the interference of the city authorities. Tilney's 30 years in office created the conditions in which the London theatre developed and Shakespeare flourished.

Old Lord Hunsdon died in 1596, tormented during his last sickness by a nightmare vision of six courtiers, 'already dead', coming 'in fire and flames' to warn him that he should prepare to join them in Purgatory.[72] His son, George Carey (1547–1603), both inherited his title and assumed patronage of his Company; and in 1597 he too became Lord Chamberlain. The influence of the Hunsdons, father and son, made the Chamberlain's Men the most successful company of the age (though no doubt the players' excellence in the quality they professed also had something to do with it); for the rest of the reign they performed more often at court than any other company, and they were always chosen to open the Christmas season of plays. It is highly likely that Shakespeare was already working with them in June 1594, when for a tentative few days they shared the inconvenient playhouse in Newington with the Admiral's Men. The usual home of the Company at this time was James Burbage's Theatre or the nearby Curtain.

During the Christmas season of 1594 the Chamberlain's Men played twice at court; and when, in March of the following year, the Queen's bureaucracy got round to paying them for these 'two several comedies or interludes', the representatives of the Company who received the payment were named: 'William Kempe, William Shakespeare and Richard Burbage, servants to the Lord Chamberlain.' It is an important moment, the first record of Shakespeare's name in the context of the theatre. Evidently by 1594 he had become a 'sharer' in the Company of the Chamberlain's Men – he was one of the principal actors and also an investor, sharing in the expenses, profits and administration of the Company. Unlike the Admiral's Men, who were ruled by Henslowe's purse, the sharers of the Chamberlain's seem to have managed their finances themselves. Shakespeare, who was to prove a skilful businessman as well as a great poet, would certainly have been useful to the Company. There were usually between eight and twelve sharers, and they were the nucleus of a big and busy organisation. Hired men, paid by the week, played smaller parts and carried out other jobs. Boy-players, apprenticed to the sharers, played the women's parts. Musicians were always needed. The gatherers collected the entrance money. The stage keepers kept the playhouse spruce and collected the apple-cores to give to the bears in the Bear Garden. The tireman looked after the costumes and properties. A vital functionary was the book-keeper, who prepared the book of the play and the actors' parts, and probably prompted too. In *A Midsummer Night's Dream* the harassed Peter Quince seems to be writer, book-keeper and tireman too for his little company; he draws up *a bill of properties such as our play wants*, and he hands each of his fellows his part – his speeches and their cues; since no actor worked from a copy of the whole play, it is not surprising that a muddled beginner like

Francis Flute should get things wrong: *you speak all your part at once, cues and all.*

Acquiring a company share was an expensive matter and it was the first of the two most significant investments of Shakespeare's life.[73] How he managed it remains a mystery. Perhaps he had saved fruitfully; but perhaps, too, he had help from Southampton or another patron; or perhaps he was able in some way to get hold of the books of his earlier plays and bring them with him – these valuable assets certainly did pass into the Company's possession at some point; or perhaps, since he himself was to become the most valuable asset of all, he simply guaranteed to keep up the supply of plays. He was in a strong position: the narrative poems had made his name as a serious writer, his plays were already popular successes, and, at 30 years old, he was no longer an upstart but a leader in a new generation of dramatists.

The brilliant wits who had transformed the art of the play during the 1580s had gone or were flickering out. In 1593 Marlowe was stabbed to death; later, a Cambridge student play pointed a sort of moral:

'Marlowe was happy in his buskin'd muse,
Alas! unhappy in his life and end.
Pity it is that wit so ill should dwell,
Wit lent from heaven, but vices sent from hell ...'

Michael Drayton, more generously, remembered that Marlowe had in him 'brave translunary things' and that his raptures 'were all air and fire'.[74] Unfortunate Thomas Kyd had at that time already been arrested and interrogated about certain ungodly papers found in his possession; he protested that they belonged to Marlowe, who had lodged with him, and he was released; but he never recovered and died in 1594. Two years later George Peele succumbed to syphilis. Lyly gave up writing, entered Parliament and began a frustrating quest for preferment (he hoped to become Master of the Revels). Nashe continued to write for a time, but soon found himself in trouble over a controversial play, and fled to exile in Yarmouth, where he was to die while still in his early thirties. Lodge, more adventurously, sailed to Brazil; back again in Europe, he became a Catholic, wrote a treatise on the plague, and lived on, a respected physician, until 1625.

Shakespeare was to continue as writer, actor and shareholder in the same Company until the end of his career, and this secure position allowed him to work without the usual pressures, to experiment and develop as his genius demanded. The fact that he was both writer and actor was one of the most important influences on his art: he was closely involved in the business, six days a week, of preparation and rehearsal in the morning and performance in the afternoon. Alexander Pope, in the preface to his edition of Shakespeare's plays (1725), observed that 'most of our Author's faults are less to be ascribed to his wrong judgment as a Poet, than to his right judgment as a Player'. That judgment was a special strength: Shakespeare knew from the inside how the theatre worked.

In an important sense his plays were probably collaborations, changing as the Company worked on them – it is interesting that Peter Quince, in his role of writer, listens to the opinions of his actors on matters of staging and even on the verse pattern of his prologue. Shakespeare wrote for particular people, and there is no doubt that his fellow actors, with their differing ideas, gifts and quirks, were an important influence on his plays. Even physical appearance must sometimes have suggested an idea: the cadaverous leanness of one of the hired men provided a way of giving individuality to the tiny parts of Romeo's Apothecary (*sharp misery had worn him to the bones*) and Robert Falconbridge in *King John*, with his legs like *riding-rods* and arms like *eel-skins stuffed*. There may, too, have been a fat man among Shakespeare's actors – or at any rate one who looked convincing under bombast padding. Today the part of Benedick in *Much Ado About Nothing* is often nimbly played, but Shakespeare seems to have had in mind a solidly-built performer who is first introduced in a cluster of jokes and puns about eating (*valiant trencherman ... excellent stomach ... stuffed man*); the joke recurs several times; and when Beatrice finally accepts his love, she says she does so to save his life, having heard that he is *in a consumption* – that he is wasting away; this quip, almost the last in the play, gets its best laugh, of course, if the actor is plump and rosy.

Most of the sharers had been Strange's Men. This company had worked for some time in amalgamation with the Admiral's Men, and it is likely that Shakespeare was then already working with them. However, in 1594, only a few months after inheriting his earldom of Derby, Ferdinando, Lord Strange died, his end shadowed by the suspicion of treason and rumours of poison, and the troupe divided. Shakespeare's fellows stayed together and made a stable company of the Chamberlain's Men; its members could certainly not be written off as rogues and vagabonds: they were more like the players described by Thomas Heywood in his *Apology for Actors* (1612) as men 'of substance, of government, of sober lives, and temperate carriages, house-keepers ...' Some of the bequests made in their wills suggest that they were not just colleagues, but friends too. John Heminges (d. 1630) managed the company finances as well as acting. He was evidently a canny businessman and accumulated a useful fortune himself. In his will he left ten shillings 'unto every of my fellows and sharers'. He was the model of a sober citizen, a trustee for his parish, and father of a huge family. Living in the same parish, where he was a churchwarden, was Henry Condell (d. 1627), who was soon to be a sharer. Like Heminges he became a rich man – he had a country house in Fulham. Shakespeare evidently had some affection for both Heminges and Condell, since he remembered them in his will with sums to buy memorial-rings. Augustine Phillips (d. 1605) was a musician as well as an actor. Another wealthy man, he left several bequests to his friends, including a silver bowl to Heminges, 30 shillings to Shakespeare and a small sum to the hired men. For Samuel Gilburne, his 'late apprentice' (presumably a boy-player) there was a touching legacy of 40 shillings together with 'my mouse-coloured velvet hose and a white taffeta doublet, a black taffeta suit, my purple cloak, sword, and dagger, and my bass viol'. Although the popular clown Will Kempe was also a sharer, he seems to have been less closely bound to this fellowship than the others. After a few years he left the Company and set off on his famous publicity stunt of dancing a morris from London to Norwich; he wrote a book about the experience, and the Mayor of Norwich gave him a small annuity, but in spite of his celebrity he never made his fortune – soon after the turn of the century he was borrowing money from Henslowe. The date of his death is not known.

The bright particular star of the Company was Richard Burbage (1571?–1619), younger son of James Burbage, who built the Theatre. He had bounded into recorded history during a notorious confrontation between James Burbage and his partner's widow, Margaret Brayne; when the confrontation became a brawl, the young Richard set about the widow's supporters with a broom-stick, and was accused of 'scornfully and disdainfully playing' with the nose of one of them.[75] The only contemporary anecdote about Shakespeare's personal life suggests a sort of jolly schoolboyish rivalry in his relationship with Burbage: it seems that he once outwitted the actor in some amorous role-play with a theatre-going lady. Along with Heminges and Condell, Burbage was one of Shakespeare's closer fellows; he too received a legacy to buy a memorial-ring. He was clearly a gifted man, not only an actor but a painter too, and well enough regarded to attract a pleasant commission. For the ceremonial Accession Day tilt on 24 March 1613 the Earl of Rutland needed an *impresa* – a paper or paste-board shield with an emblematic design and a riddling motto. These ornamental devices often drew admiration, and many hung in the Shield Gallery in Whitehall Palace. Rutland, prepared to lay out generously to get an effective *impresa*, commissioned Burbage to make and paint it, and Shakespeare to compose the motto, and he paid each of them 44 shillings in gold – more than a hired man of the Company could expect to earn in a busy month.

As an actor Burbage was much admired. His death in March 1619 so saddened the Earl of Pembroke that, bidden to accompany the French ambassador to the playhouse, he found he could not endure to go there 'so soon after the loss of my old acquaintance'. It was for this great actor that Shakespeare certainly wrote the tremendous parts of Richard Crookback, Hamlet, Lear, the grieved Moor Othello; and he presumably played other central characters too,

'Upon a time when Burbage played Richard III there was a citizen grew so far in liking with him, that before she went from the play she appointed him to come that night unto her by the name of Richard III. Shakespeare overhearing their conclusion went before, was entertained, and at his game ere Burbage came. Then message being brought that Richard III was at the door, Shakespeare caused return to be made that William the Conqueror was before Richard III. Shakespeare's name William.'

DIARY OF JOHN MANNINGHAM,
13 MARCH 1602

perhaps even the whole extraordinary range from ardent Romeo to brooding Prospero. A writer of the next century, who could never have seen Burbage act, knew of his reputation for 'wholly transforming himself into his part' and never resuming his own identity, not even in the tiring-house, until the play was done. The same writer recognised the productive symbiosis of dramatist and player: 'It was the happiness of the actors of those times to have such poets ... to instruct them; and no less of those poets to have such docile and excellent actors to act their plays.'[76]

Working with these and other Company men – William Sly, Richard Cowley, the comedian Thomas Pope – Shakespeare was

The actor Richard Burbage (1571?–1619)

able to create the masterpieces of his early maturity. *Romeo and Juliet* and *A Midsummer Night's Dream* were written close together, as several correspondences between them show.[77] In both plays Shakespeare's lyric note, the 'honey-flowing vein' of the poems, is very much in evidence, though he was already exploring other kinds of dramatic language. *Romeo and Juliet* begins with a sonnet and ends with a sestet (a favourite pattern for love poetry, the stanza form of *Venus and Adonis*), and for half its length the play is in effect a lyric comedy of hopeful love. The language of the lovers themselves is full of pretty word-play and the imagery of moonlight and birdsong; their first meeting involves a symmetrically shared love-sonnet. Shakespeare manages a delicate tension between ecstasy and absurdity; indeed he makes Mercutio explicitly ridicule the language of the sonneteers:

Speak but one rhyme and I am satisfied.
Cry but 'Ay me!' Pronounce but 'love' and 'dove' ...

Capulet and the Nurse, inhabitants of a different world, speak a different kind of dramatic verse; though it is still artfully organised it seems in its rushing energy to have absorbed the diction and patterns of living speech, for instance when the baffled Capulet rages at Juliet's refusal to marry Paris:

How, how, how, how – chopped logic? What is this?
'Proud', and 'I thank you', and 'I thank you not',
And yet 'not proud'? Mistress minion, you,
Thank me no thankings, nor proud me no prouds ...

In *A Midsummer Night's Dream* Egeus, that other father of a self-willed daughter, flings out his anger with similar stuttering repetitions. As the tragedy of *Romeo and Juliet* darkens, the language of the lovers becomes more intense, and the lyric manner is left to the unlucky conventional lover Paris – his farewell to Juliet as she lies in the Capulet tomb is a touching sestet.

A Midsummer Night's Dream is a finished masterpiece: Shakespeare never wrote anything quite like it again. The four narrative strands, effortlessly controlled and interwoven, belong to different expressive worlds. The lovers, of course, speak in the lyric mode, and again there is the delicate balance between charm and absurdity. The long episode of their four-sided quarrel is a display of stylistic fireworks, beginning with two passionate sestets, developing into rapid rhyming couplets, graduating as the speakers grow heated into vigorous blank verse, and reaching high comedy when the two boy-players, one tall and one little, resort to frank insults. The interlude performed by Quince's troupe of Mechanicals is Ovid's tale of Pyramus and Thisbe transformed into a hilariously silly version of the *Romeo* story. This miniature masterpiece is a parody of the histrionic excesses of older plays; but Shakespeare, a daring parodist, was mocking himself too – he was, after all, quite prepared to use the same stylistic devices in his own serious work. When Pyramus apostrophises night he seems to be echoing Helena's exhausted words earlier in the play: *O weary night, O long and tedious night.* The comic change of tense when Pyramus believes Thisbe dead (*... which is – no, no, which was – the fairest dame*) anticipates a trick used to poignant effect in *Julius Caesar* when Titinius sees the dead Cassius. Like Pyramus, Hamlet superfluously announces his own death, and murdered Richard II imagines his soul mounting skywards. Even the repetitive (and alliterative) padding out of a line can appear at a moment of heart-searching tragedy: *O Desdemon! Dead Desdemon! Dead! O! O!*[78]

For the fairies (who also make a cameo appearance in *Romeo and Juliet*) Shakespeare developed his most musical diction yet, delectably varied in its rhythms and patterns, glimmering with image and allusion. Within a few years there was to be something of a vogue for poems of fancy about the miniature fairy world, and the more elaborate Jacobean imaginings show, by contrast, just how perfectly proportioned Shakespeare's fantasy was. William Browne's Oberon dines on 'larded mites', lady-bird pie, roasted flies and a butterfly 'kill'd that day'; Michael Drayton's Oberon, who lives in a palace with 'windows of the eyes of cats', wears fish-scale armour and a helmet made of a beetle's head with a horse's hair for a plume.[79] Shakespeare too has plenty of fun with the wings of painted butterflies, sweet musk-roses, dewberries and spangled starlight sheen, but his dream is firmly planted in country earth.

The chronicles of English history continued to feed Shakespeare's imagination at this time. *Richard II*[80] was the first play in what was to become another tetralogy of histories, taking his earlier narrative back to its beginning in the events leading to the forced abdication and murder of King Richard – the high crime which set off the long contention of York and Lancaster. The tone of *Richard II* is controlled and ceremonial, very unlike that of the violent and discursive *Henry VI* plays. Its most famous passage, John of Gaunt's celebration of England as *This royal throne of kings*, was anthologised almost at once: in 1600 it appeared, truncated, misquoted and attributed to Drayton, in a miscellany called *England's Parnassus: or the choicest Flowers of our Modern Poets*. In this shortened version it has remained famous as an exultantly patriotic poem; in the context of the play, however, the effect is bleak – the lines are part of Gaunt's lament for *this dear, dear land* which is *now leas'd out … like to a tenement or pelting farm*. The ancient certainty was that the monarch is God's deputy:

Not all the water in the rough rude sea
Can wash the balm from an anointed king.

But the old order is changing: *tradition, form, and ceremonious duty* are giving way to the new realities. The gardeners in their choric scene quietly observe what is happening: the *sea-walled garden* of England is choked with weeds, its wholesome herbs *swarming with caterpillars*; and the king *hath now himself met with the fall of leaf*.

This was sensitive material. The climax of the play is the scene where Richard is forced to abdicate by Bolingbroke, who, as Henry IV, becomes the first Lancastrian king. For a moment the adversaries both have their hands on the crown, and the stage picture is a visible metaphor for the transience of kingly power. This scene was never printed in Elizabeth's lifetime, though the play went into three editions. We do not know whether the censor intervened, or whether the caution of the Company, or of the printer, kept the scene from publication; but the implications of the play were clearly dangerous, and within a few years a performance of it was to bring the Company close to disaster. Not until the fourth edition (1608), when a new monarch was on the throne, was it possible at last to include, as some copies of the title-page put it, *the Parliament Scene, and the deposing of King Richard*.

Although *King John*[81] is an independent play, unconnected with the main cycle of histories, it inevitably shares some of the familiar ideas. However, the energetic narrative is concerned less with the sanctity of kingship than with the cynicism of power. John's claim to the throne is presented as doubtful – as his formidable mother brazenly asserts, *strong possession* is more significant than *right*; but since he also stands for English defiance against the aggression of the French and the machinations of the Papacy, it is not easy for the patriotic spectator to decide whether to hiss him as a villain or cheer him on as a champion. His plan to murder his little nephew, Prince Arthur, brings an authentic shiver of wickedness as he and his henchman Hubert split a pentameter into sinister fragments:

JOHN	*Death.*
HUBERT	*My lord.*
JOHN	*A grave.*
HUBERT	*He shall not live.*
JOHN	*Enough.*
	I could be merry now. Hubert, I love thee.

Though John is the centre of the story, he is not in himself a very interesting figure, and greater dramatic excitement is generated by other characters and episodes; for instance, by the scene where Hubert intends to burn out Arthur's eyes and is turned away from that brutality by the graceful rhetoric of the child's pleading; or the astounding moment when Arthur leaps to his death from the wall of his prison; or the unhinged grief of his mother, Constance – Shakespeare was clearly able to call on a boy-player who could tear a passion to tatters. The most interesting character is Philip the Bastard, a gleeful sceptic who is clear-eyed about the nature of John's rule, but also understands the *vast confusion* that must be the consequence of rebellion: when things fall apart he remains loyal. His robust voice closes the play with that note of sombre patriotism that is so frequently heard in Shakespeare's histories:

> *This England never did, nor never shall*
> *Lie at the proud foot of a conqueror*
> *But when it first did help to wound itself …*

The middle years of the decade were not comfortable. As well as the great national troubles of threatening war, high taxation and unemployment, it seemed that the elements themselves had turned against the dear, dear land. The cruelly unseasonable summer of 1594 began a weather pattern which was to last for some years – summers that were 'wonderful cold like winter' with flooding rains, so that 'many did sit by the fire'.[82] Harvests were damaged and profiteers hoarded grain; there was serious distress. The playhouse listeners must have shivered to hear the boy-player speak Titania's evocation of the disordered seasons, a too-familiar picture of drowned fields, diseased flocks and the green corn that *hath rotted ere his youth attained a beard*. In Stratford the troubles were made more severe by two great fires which devastated the town just a year apart; since, with a strange neatness, both occurred on Sundays, the preachers were certain that God had punished the impious town for profaning the Sabbath. John Shakespeare's house was untouched, but buildings nearby in Henley Street were destroyed; it was said that the damage as a whole amounted to £12,000. In London there were food riots, and the authorities reacted savagely by executing several of the rioters. The Lord Mayor requested the closing of the playhouses, claiming that 'the late stir and mutinous attempt' of apprentices and others to create disorder arose out of 'infection from these and like places'.[83] The Chamberlain's Men took to the road. If Shakespeare went with them, he would probably not have known for some time that his 11-year-old son, Hamnet, was dying in Stratford. He was buried there on 11 August 1596.

Reputation and Profit 1596–9

Elizabethan households knew too well how fragile a child's life could be: about a third of all Stratford children died before they reached their teens – Mary Shakespeare bore eight children, three of them little girls who never grew to adulthood. It is not unreasonable to imagine that Shakespeare's sense of loss might have been reflected in his writing, perhaps that personal grief deepened his sense of tragedy: biographers have found echoes of it in the Sonnets, with their intimations of mortality, and in *Hamlet*.[84] In fact, however, nobody knows how Shakespeare was affected by this death of a son he had been able to see only seldom. The relationship of life and art is not always obvious: it is perfectly possible that Shakespeare was at his happiest when, in a fine frenzy, he was working on a great and painful tragedy, and gloomier when he was trudging through the necessary quips and complications of a funny play.[85] In the years following Hamnet's death Shakespeare was writing some of his richest and most affirmative comedy.

He had certainly not lost touch with Stratford, and two important developments at this time ensured that he was not without honour, of a sort, in his own country. John Shakespeare's application to the College of Heralds for a coat of arms had been shelved some 20 years earlier; now it was revived, presumably by his son, and in the autumn of 1596 the grant was made at last. Years later, when a fuss blew up about the inappropriate granting of arms, the Shakespeare grant was specifically cited; but in fact it

Shakespear if Player
by Garter

A sketch of Shakespeare's coat of arms, granted in 1596

was not unusual. William Harrison dryly observed that any person who can 'bear the port, charge and countenance of a gentleman … shall for money have a coat and arms bestowed upon him by heralds' who customarily 'pretend antiquity and service'.[86] Between 1560 and 1640, the College of Heralds made 6,000 grants of this kind.[87] The Shakespeare coat of arms is both grand and austere: a plain gold shield with, diagonally across it, on a black band, a gold spear silver-tipped; above the shield, as 'crest or cognisance', a silver falcon displays its wings and supports (or shakes) another silver-tipped spear. John Shakespeare could now boast, like the Old Shepherd of *The Winter's Tale*, that his *sons and daughters will all be gentlemen born.*

The other, and more material, indication of Shakespeare's continuing interest in Stratford was his purchase in 1597 of one of the most important houses in the town, New Place. It had been built a century earlier by Sir Hugh Clopton (d. 1496), sometime

Lord Mayor of London and one of the great Stratford worthies. Clopton's 'great house' was badly in need of restoration when Shakespeare bought it, but it was still an imposing property and in the heart of things: only the width of a lane separated it from the Guild Chapel where John Shakespeare had presided as Bailiff. It was shielded from the street by a brick wall in which there was a porch leading to 'a small kind of green court'.[88] The house was large (it had ten fireplaces) and there were orchards and gardens; there, according to tradition, Shakespeare planted a mulberry tree which in time came to be seen as a venerable relic of the poet. In the 1780s the owner of the house, Francis Gastrell, irritated by the number of visiting enthusiasts, chopped the tree down and sold the wood to an enterprising trader who carved it into a suspiciously large number of Shakespeare souvenirs.[89] Soon afterwards Gastrell demolished the house itself, and only a few traces remain. Where the building once stood there are now pleasant gardens; the exhausted pilgrim in search of Shakespeare can still tarry in the mulberry shade – in the Great Garden is another old tree, said to be a distant relative of Shakespeare's own.

In Stratford Shakespeare was, it seems, prudently preparing for a settled and comfortable future. In London, on the other hand, his circumstances suggest a sense of impermanence. Although it was there that he made his name and spent his working years, he bought no London property until 1613. He lived in lodgings, though not austerely (his goods were assessed at the comfortable value of £5), and he occasionally changed his address. He was not meticulous about paying his taxes, and demands for outstanding sums followed him for some time. By 1596 he was living in the parish of St Helen's, Bishopsgate, a little to the south of where Liverpool Street Station now stands; it was a thoroughly respectable neighbourhood, within the wall but not far from the Shoreditch playhouses. Soon afterwards he moved south of the river, probably to the Liberty of the Clink, near the Rose, a crowded, low-lying area crossed by many ditches, and still known at that time for its taverns and whorehouses. More than a third of the householders in the neighbourhood were watermen.[90]

Shakespeare was probably living there when he was caught up in an unpleasant situation which has never been fully explained. A goldsmith named Francis Langley, who owned land on Bankside, proposed to build another playhouse there, despite the articulate opposition of the Lord Mayor. At some point Langley quarrelled with a rich, corrupt and bullying magistrate, William Gardiner, who had jurisdiction in the area. Langley petitioned for sureties of the peace against Gardiner and his stepson William Wayte, on the grounds that he feared death or injury; Wayte retaliated by craving sureties on the same grounds not only against Langley, but also against William Shakespeare (and others). The most generous interpretation is that Shakespeare, rather than actually threatening death or injury, was merely supporting a friend; and he may also have been involved in some way with Langley's playhouse plans. In any case no more was heard of the affair, and by 1596, despite the Lord Mayor's protests and Gardiner's opposition, Langley's new playhouse, the Swan, was in business.

A Dutch tourist, Johannes de Witt, visited London at this time and marvelled at the splendid theatres, especially the Swan, which he considered *omnium prestantissimum* – the finest of them all. He fancied that it resembled a Roman theatre, and to illustrate this idea he made a now famous sketch of the interior – it survives only as a pen-and-ink copy made by a contemporary and countryman of his. It is not detailed, and there are puzzling features, but it is of incomparable importance as the only contemporary depiction of a public playhouse interior; through it we can glimpse the sort of working conditions that fostered Shakespeare's craft.

The following labels appear within the sketch:

tectum

porticus

sedilia

orchestra

ingressus

mimorum aedes:

proscaenium

planities sive arena

Ex observationibus Londinensibus Johannis de Witt

The Swan Theatre, in a pen-and-ink copy of the sketch made by
Johannes de Witt

The familiar features are there. The raised stage juts out into
the yard, which is empty in the sketch but during a performance
would be crowded with perhaps a thousand groundlings – those
who could afford only the basic entrance charge of one penny and
stood to hear the play. Round the yard are the three covered galleries
where those who were prepared to pay an extra penny sat protected

from the weather. Behind the stage is the tiring-house, labelled *mimorum aedes*, the house of the actors, where the players attired themselves. They made their exits and their entrances through the double doors set in the tiring-house wall. Above the doors is a gallery, perhaps containing the lords' rooms where the grandest auditors sat; this gallery could be pressed into service for the action of the play – actors sometimes appeared *above*. The two fat pillars support the 'cover' or canopy over the stage (a little trouble with perspective in the sketch); this canopy, often called 'the heavens' and richly painted on its underside, was not only a protection for the stage, but also an element in the iconography of the playhouse – in *Macbeth* this symbolism has an ominous colouring:

> *Thou seest the heavens, as troubled with man's act,*
> *Threatens his bloody stage …*

This little drawing, plain and diagrammatic though it is, conveys something of the life of the playhouses Shakespeare knew: a banner is flying from the tiring-house tower, and a trumpeter is announcing a performance which seems already to have begun – on stage a courtier is bowing histrionically before two boy-players in their farthingales.

One of the great comedies of this period was *The Merchant of Venice*,[91] soon to be entered in the Stationers' Register as 'otherwise called the Jew of Venice', as if Shylock was already beginning his take-over of the imagination, displacing the eponymous Merchant, Antonio, at the emotional centre of the play. Occasionally in Shakespeare's work there are startling reminders of how remote the values of his world can seem to us now: Shylock must be the most striking of these challenges to modern sensibilities. There were not very many

Jews in Shakespeare's London; some were Italian musicians, like the family of Emilia Lanier, or immigrants from Spain and Portugal; most were converts to Christianity or conformed to the requirements of Elizabeth's Church. The most famous was the Queen's physician, the unfortunate Doctor Lopez; a victim of court faction, he was accused of treason and in 1594 appallingly put to death in a thunder of popular hatred, protesting on the scaffold that 'he loved the Queen as well as he loved Jesus Christ'.[92]

The two or three references to Jews in Shakespeare's other plays suggest that his attitude was probably that of his time – if not hatred, at best an easy dismissal of them: they are conventionally imagined as heartless, and as aliens in a Christian world: the *liver of blaspheming Jew*, along with other infidel titbits (nose of Turk, Tartar's lips), is an ingredient in the bubbling cauldron of Macbeth's witches. An authoritative modern study of Shylock[93] argues that Shakespeare seems not to have known much about Judaism; the Jewish touches in the play suggest only superficial understanding; he invests Shylock with a kind of stereotypical stage-Judaism. However, Shakespeare added to his stereotype enough complexity to convey a sense of fierce life: in Shylock's most famous utterance, he seems now to speak for all persecuted peoples. This is not to suggest that Shakespeare was uncommonly liberal in a modern sense, but rather that his dramatic imagination was empathetic, reaching out in sometimes unexpected ways.

The contempt and coarse mockery shown by the play's Christians prevent a simplistic tilting of the moral balance in their favour. The last Act, therefore, can seem an anti-climax if it is not allowed full voice. Order and harmony are restored in the imagery of love, moonlight and, one of Shakespeare's favourite symbols, music, which evokes the divine ordering of the spheres and the harmony which *is in immortal souls*. Returning to Belmont, Portia hears the music of her house and sees the candle in her hall shining like *a good deed in a naughty world*. There is surely no intentional irony. One of the good deeds of the play is the sparing of Shylock's life (in that, at least, he is more fortunate than Doctor Lopez). The decision that he should *presently become a Christian*, usually seen now as a gratuitous humiliation, would certainly have seemed to Shakespeare's audience another *good deed* – a practical demonstration of *the quality of mercy*. Every Good Friday Elizabeth's churches asked God to have mercy on 'Jews, Turks, infidels and heretics', to take from them all hardness of heart, and to fetch them home to His flock 'that they may be saved among the remnant of the true Israelites'.

Shakespeare continued to work on his cycle of histories. The two *Henry IV* plays,[94] picking up the chronicle after the death of Richard II, show a significant advance in his ambitious mastery of his material, and in his control of tone, the 'interchange of seriousness and merriment' which Doctor Johnson saw as one of his distinctive characteristics. In this new kind of history play, human comedy is not merely incidental but makes an elaborate counterpoint to the great events: while rebellion shakes the throne of Bolingbroke, now King Henry IV, his unthrifty son Prince Hal, with his gang of Eastcheap companions, enjoys his own kind of rebellion against order. The most beguiling of them is, of course, Sir John Falstaff. This extraordinary character brought instant popularity for *1 Henry IV*: it went into more published editions during Shakespeare's lifetime than any of his plays except *Richard III*. Audiences have always adored Falstaff, not only because he is funny, but also because he is subversive; his is the play's great rebellion: he subverts order, morality, sobriety, truthfulness; he rebels against the law, against the demands of honour – *What is honour? A word.* Although there is plenty of fun to be had from his girth (*How long is't ago, Jack, since thou sawest thine own knee?*), the richest source of humour in his scenes is their verbal inventiveness, which is in no way constrained by being woven into Shakespeare's most elaborately contrived prose.

The second play is less genial than the first. The rebellion, which had blazed with its own fierce honour, is defeated not by honest warfare but by a coldly efficient trap. The King is failing. There is a sense of time running out. Falstaff, advised by his whore to patch up his old body for heaven, begs her not to speak like a death's head: *do not bid me remember mine end*. The most original episodes are those set in Gloucestershire, where Justice Shallow and his cousin Silence gossip about country affairs and reminisce about old friends now dead: *Death, as the Psalmist saith, is certain to all; all shall die. How a good yoke of bullocks at Stamford fair?* In this calm backwater Falstaff's wit seems cynical and cruel.

The grave and beautiful reconciliation scene between Hal and his dying father draws the threads of the chronicle together, looking back to the beginning of the story (the *indirect crook'd ways* by which Henry gained the crown), and also preparing for the next chapter: Hal will rule by just inheritance. The climactic arrival of the new order is not comfortable. The news of the King's death reaches Falstaff as he is sampling last year's pippins with a dish of caraway in Shallow's orchard, and he dashes to London to welcome in the triumph of misrule: *I know the young King is sick for me. Let us take any man's horses – the laws of England are at my commandment.* Hal's rejection of his old friend is both inevitable and shocking, especially as behind its cold finality sounds a faint echo of the old wit. In the Epilogue to the play, Shakespeare gave his audience an assurance: *if you be not too much cloyed with fat meat, our humble author will continue the story with Sir John in it.* But he changed his mind: though he did continue the chronicle, it was without Sir John.

However, he did indeed write one more Falstaff play, of a very different kind, and he may well have broken off from work on the histories to do so. According to a well-known tradition, first recorded in 1702, it was the Queen herself who commanded him to write *The Merry Wives of Windsor*,[95] and moreover to do it in 14 days; a slightly later version of the story explained why – she wished to see the fat knight in love. Unfortunately there is no evidence of any personal contact between Elizabeth and Shakespeare, and no record of her reaction to any of his plays. However, passages from the festive last Act could well have been part of the entertainment at the Garter Feast on St George's Day, 23 April 1597; one of the new knights was Lord Hunsdon, patron of Shakespeare's Company.

The Falstaff of this jolly play is in every way (except the physical) a slighter figure than his other self of the histories, but he is still unscrupulously cynical, and certainly not in love; he woos the two merry ladies not for their hearts but for their money: *they shall be my East and West Indies, and I will trade to them both*. Yet this comedy is much less cynical in its effect than the Falstaff histories. His adventures in adulterous seduction end in farce, and his punishment is no worse than fittingly absurd. This is Shakespeare's only comedy of middle-class life, and the harmless gossiping and quarrelling of the burghers and their comfortable wives make an affectionate portrait of the sort of environment he knew: perhaps it is merely coincidence that in the play the pert child who is so quick at his lesson is called William – and the pretty girl who marries for love is Anne.

Shakespeare's growing fame is suggested by the fact that in 1598 his name at last began to appear, presumably as a useful selling-point, on the title-pages of his plays; and that same year produced what could be seen as the first critical appraisal of Shakespeare the writer. In his *Palladis Tamia: Wit's Treasury*, Francis Meres (1565–1647) included 'A Comparative Discourse of Our English

Poets', a not very discriminating list in which Shakespeare's name figures frequently (though not as frequently as Michael Drayton's). Meres cites him as one of those by whom 'the English tongue is mightily enriched and gorgeously invested in rare ornaments'; he praises him as a mellifluous poet in whom 'the sweet witty soul of Ovid lives'; and to illustrate his excellence in both comedy and tragedy he lists all the plays Shakespeare had written by that time, except *The Shrew* and *Henry VI*. He includes the mysterious *Love's Labour's Won*, a name which also appears on a bookseller's list from 1603. This may be an alternative title for another play, but it could, more intriguingly, belong to one which has disappeared. Since so many of the plays written at this time have since been lost, it would not be surprising if one of Shakespeare's was among the casualties – indeed, it may not be the only one.

Towards the end of the 1590s, and after Meres had made his list, Shakespeare wrote another great comedy of love, and he also completed his second cycle of histories. *Much Ado About Nothing*[96] is one of his boldest experiments in the interchange of seriousness and merriment. One of its two contrasting love-stories is almost a preliminary sketch for *Othello*, with a motivelessly malignant villain and an innocent lady falsely accused of unchastity. The other is virtuoso comedy, the *merry war* of Beatrice and Benedick, for which Shakespeare developed to a dagger-sharp point the technique of his prose dialogue, with its supple rhythms and inventive imagery. At the edge of the story is the town constable, Dogberry, an irresistible part designed for Will Kempe – indeed, it was the last part Shakespeare wrote for the famous clown. It is thought that Kempe had a gift for improvisation, which, as Shakespeare knew, can be a dangerous talent: Hamlet complains of the clowns who speak more than is set down for them and set *barren spectators* to laughing, though meanwhile *some necessary question of the play be then to be considered*. Shakespeare actually exploited the danger: the resolution of the most pressingly necessary question of *Much Ado* is delayed by nothing but the slow wit and unstoppable tongue of Kempe's Dogberry. The whole play is a sprightly game, full of tricks and disguises, overhearing and hiding; and it ends with a dance.

In spite of its popularity, *Henry V*, last play in the second history cycle, has not always found critical favour.[97] Some commentators, preferring Shakespeare the crypto-modern, have dismissed it as merely conventional in its patriotism, and therefore remote from the serious concerns of the other histories.[98] There is indeed an important element of idealised patriotism, especially in the longer Folio version; the play was written at a time of *expectation in the air*, of furious preparation against a renewed threat of Spanish invasion. Conscription was rising sharply, and although players were exempt since they were thought to serve the Queen, there was plenty of opportunity for impressment among theatre-goers.[99] The Spanish threat was not the only danger. In March 1599 the Earl of Essex, accompanied by, among others, Southampton, set off on his campaign to suppress Tyrone's rebellion in Ireland, and his departure from London was through a press of enthusiastic crowds, *plebeians swarming at his heels*. The Chorus in *Henry V* loyally hopes that in time *the General of our gracious Empress* will return from Ireland with *rebellion broached on his sword* – Shakespeare does not usually favour this kind of explicit topical allusion.

However, the celebration of ideal heroism is complicated, even undermined, by a sense of the reality of war, of *rainy marching in the painful field*, of *waste and desolation*, of horrors committed by *the blind and bloody soldier*. During the uneasy night before the great battle, ordinary unheroic men talk quietly about the coming slaughter and the *heavy reckoning* the King who brought them to it will have to make. This serious conversation is unusual in Shakespeare, who more often depicts the common man as stupid, coarse or comic, like the Eastcheap gang, whose continuing story makes a different kind of sardonic comment on the epic events. They have joined the war for what they can get out of it, and by the end all but one are dead. Falstaff, of course, is not there, but he is given a funny and touching valediction in which Mistress Quickly describes how, as he lay dying of a *fracted* heart, he fumbled with the sheets and (perhaps remembering the comfortable Psalm) *babbled of green fields*. With *Henry V* Shakespeare filled in the last gap in his great eight-play chronicle. The King, in his prayer before Agincourt, looks back to the murder of Richard which began the story. The Epilogue looks forward to the next reign, reminding the listeners that the hero-king is to die young, and that under his successor, the infant Henry VI, England will begin once more to bleed – the cruel story *which oft our stage hath shown*.

Shakespeare may not actually have meant Falstaff to babble of green fields. In the Folio the passage is mysterious: *his Nose was as sharpe as a Pen, and a Table of greene fields*. The phrase now usually accepted is a conjectural emendation, perhaps the most famous in Shakespeare, made by Lewis Theobald. Though Doctor Johnson attacked him as 'a man of narrow comprehension', ignorant, petulant and ostentatious, Theobald has his immortality: his emendation (one of many that he made) is now irreplaceably part of Shakespeare's work – and of the Falstaff myth.

Shakespeare was becoming not only well-known but also moderately wealthy: at any rate, Stratford notables seem to have thought him prosperous enough to have funds to spare – so it appears from the correspondence between the lawyer Abraham Sturley and Richard Quiney, son of John Shakespeare's friend Adrian Quiney. The town was still suffering from the years of dearth and the two great fires, and times were hard. Some hoarding of grain had gone on, to the fury of the needier townsfolk, and a survey of February 1598 revealed that Shakespeare had stored ten quarters of malt, not as much, admittedly, as some other men 'of good livelihood' but still a prudent stock. In October Richard Quiney was in London to seek official relief for the distressed town, and, finding himself in debt, wrote to Shakespeare as his 'loving good friend and countryman' asking for a loan of £30. This is the only surviving letter to Shakespeare, and since it was discovered, a folded scrap, among Quiney's own papers it is possible that it was never sent. We do not know whether Shakespeare lent him the money – Quiney's mission was a success and his expenses were paid by the government.[100]

But while Shakespeare the Stratford householder was prospering, his Company in London had problems. Hunsdon's death in 1596 had lost them a friend at court, and it was some months before his son was appointed Chamberlain and they could resume their familiar name. In the interval between the Hunsdons the Lord Chamberlain was William Brooke, Lord Cobham, no great friend to the Company. Shakespeare soon managed to offend him, perhaps on purpose. The disreputable fat knight of *1 Henry IV* was at first given the name of Sir John Oldcastle, a name which belonged to a historical figure, a celebrated Wycliffite martyr who happened to be one of Cobham's ancestors. There was perhaps some similar mockery in *Merry Wives*, where Cobham's family name of Brooke featured absurdly. It seems that Cobham or his family did take offence, and to avoid a fuss both names were changed: Brooke became Broome and Oldcastle became, of course, Falstaff.

More serious than this minor flurry was the storm that blew up over a play called *The Isle of Dogs*, presented by Pembroke's Men at the Swan. When the authorities judged it to be lewd, seditious and slanderous, all the companies suffered. In July 1597 the Privy Council sent an order to the Justices of Middlesex and Surrey (including the appalling Gardiner) requiring that the playhouses should be 'plucked down'. Fortunately this order was never carried out, but they remained closed throughout the summer.

Nashe, involved as one of the authors, fled from London; another, the brilliant and provocative Ben Jonson (1572–1637), spent the summer in Marshalsea Prison; he was a coming man, soon to be Shakespeare's greatest rival and a not-uncritical admirer. The Chamberlain's Men went on their travels – a situation which, as Shakespeare later made Hamlet observe, was not helpful either for their *reputation* or for their *profit*.

But the Company's greatest trouble had arisen because James Burbage's aging Theatre stood on ground which had been leased for 21 years; the lease was due to expire in April 1597, and the landowner, Giles Allen, was reluctant to renew it. While he carried on a long game of cat and mouse with Burbage, the Company was performing at the Curtain and perhaps the Swan. Clearly a more stable arrangement was needed. In 1596 Burbage bought a property in the precinct of Blackfriars and converted it to create an indoor playhouse very different from the Theatre – small, intimate and candle-lit. Had this playhouse become the Company's home in 1596, as Burbage seems to have intended, the change would have had a profound effect on Shakespeare's development as a dramatist (and on the whole story of dramatic literature). But the plan was not allowed to succeed. The Blackfriars residents, fearing that a 'common playhouse' would be 'a very great annoyance and trouble', bringing 'lewd persons' into their exclusive precinct and disrupting Divine Service with 'the noise of the drums and trumpets', petitioned the Privy Council, and Burbage was stopped. Among the petitioners were Shakespeare's friend Richard Field and Lord Hunsdon, the Company's own patron. Burbage died in February 1597, and the conduct of his affairs passed to his sons, Cuthbert and the actor Richard.

By 1598 the Company's crisis was acute. Giles Allen refused to budge. The Blackfriars playhouse, purchased, as the Burbage brothers later claimed, 'at extreme rates' and converted 'with great charge and trouble',[101] was useless for the time being. Faced with an apparently insoluble difficulty, they decided on a buccaneering manoeuvre. The ground on which the Theatre stood was Allen's, but the building itself was arguably theirs. On 28 December 1598, a night of snow and brutal cold, the Burbage brothers, with the carpenter Peter Street and a gang of workmen, began the process of taking the playhouse to pieces and carrying it away.

There is the playhouse now 1599–1603

Giles Allen had hoped to get his hands on the Theatre and 'convert
the wood and timber thereof to better use', but he was away from
London during its demolition, and there was nothing he could
do except take his anger to the courts. He accused the Burbages
of acting 'in very outrageous, violent and riotous sort', of using
'many unlawful and offensive weapons' against the peaceable
farmers who tried to stop them, of scaring the neighbours, of
trampling the grass.[102] And indeed they had not indisputably kept
on the windy side of the law. But he never received satisfaction,
though the dispute nagged on for some years and even reached
the Star Chamber. Meanwhile the precious bones of the Theatre
were transported across the river to Southwark, where Cuthbert
Burbage had negotiated the lease of a plot of land from the lawyer
Nicholas Brend. There Peter Street did indeed put the old timbers
to better use: with them he built the most famous of the Elizabethan playhouses, the first Globe.

To meet the costs of this venture the Chamberlain's Men
developed a new system of theatre finance, a syndicate of share-
holders, or 'housekeepers', drawn from the Company. The Burbage
brothers each had a quarter interest; the remaining half interest
was divided in equal proportions among five 'deserving men',
Shakespeare, Heminges, Phillips, Pope and Kempe. All the house-
keepers except Cuthbert Burbage were Company men: for the first
time the players had a financial stake in the playhouse itself. It

was the second of the two most significant investments of Shakespeare's career: he was now not only actor, writer and sharer in the Company, but also a housekeeper with a 10 per cent interest in the playhouse; his position was as secure as it could be in the volatile world of the London theatre.

Although about half of his plays were written for other theatres, it is the Globe which is irreplaceably fixed in the imagination as Shakespeare's playhouse. It was a polygonal building (from a distance it probably looked circular) and open to the skies, though the galleries and tiring-house round the perimeter were roofed with thatch. Performances were signalled by the flying of a flag with, according to tradition, the device of Hercules bearing the world, the globe, on his shoulders; its motto was *Totus mundus agit histrionem* – or, in Shakespeare's famous variation, *All the world's a stage*.

The main features of the interior were basically those of the Swan drawing, though no doubt there were differences. It was handsomely decorated, the wood of the pillars painted to represent marble. There may have been a third entrance on to the stage – Shakespeare's plays seem to require one. A curtain or hanging could probably be drawn across one or more of the doorways, creating a place of concealment or discovery: Polonius could hide there, the curtain becoming the arras through which Hamlet stabs him to death; Prospero draws the curtain and *discovers Ferdinand and Miranda playing at chess*. There was certainly a trap-door in the stage: in *Hamlet* it is Ophelia's grave; the Clown stands in it, digging up skulls and jowling them to the ground. Earlier in the play the Ghost of Old Hamlet returns to his purgatorial prison-house by way of the trap, so that he is well-placed for the stage direction of a few lines later: *The Ghost cries under the Stage*. The space beneath was useful for supernatural manoeuvres: in *Antony and Cleopatra*, soldiers on watch by night *place themselves in every corner of the stage*, and as they stand guard gradually become aware of mysterious and other-worldly sounds: *music of the hautboys is heard under the stage.*

There is still uncertainty about these and other particular features of the Globe, but at least three essential conditions of performance in the Elizabethan public playhouse are certain enough; they are fundamentally different from the conventions of a typical modern theatre, and they were crucial in shaping and developing Shakespeare's art. First, the background to every performance was the tiring-house, and, apart from occasional variation in hangings or furniture, it was always the same. There was no specially-designed set to identify location or convey atmosphere; every play, every scene, had the same familiar architectural setting, which was simply ignored if necessary by the selective eyes of the audience. Secondly, the stage which thrust out from this background projected right into the audience; groundlings stood on three sides of it, close enough to pluck an actor by the cloak. On this broad and deep platform the effect was three-dimensional, and with no naturalistic scene-changes the action was swift and continuous. Telling juxtapositions were possible: the courtiers of *As You Like It* prepare a banquet for the Duke *under this tree*, and there it remains, still visible to the audience, while on the other side of the stage (in 'another part of the forest', as editors have sometimes put it) old Adam is fainting with hunger: *I can go no further. O, I die for food.*

A third, and specially significant, characteristic of the Shakespearean public playhouse is that the performances took place in the chancy daylight of the London afternoon, which embraced audience and players alike. There was no cosy darkness in which the audience could escape the immediacy of the play, no helpful illumination for the stage and the players. Indeed the positioning of the Globe ensured that the acting area was always in the shade.[103] It cannot always have been easy to see the play comfortably; quite apart from the shaded daylight there must have been moments when a player's expressive gesture or reaction was masked from some of the spectators by another actor or by the stage posts. Shakespeare's technique, deployed again and again, was to use words to direct the eye towards significant details – and at the same time to give them interpretative colouring: to Beatrice's secretive movement *like a lapwing ... close by the ground*, or to Cicero glancing about him with ferret and fiery eyes, or to Cassio's gallantry as he kisses three fingers to Desdemona.[104] Although Elizabethan audiences certainly enjoyed visual excitements, and Shakespeare sometimes provided them, in the playhouse it was the sense of hearing that mattered – often there was, at least by the theatrical standards of our own day, little to see. The Globe has rightly been described as an acoustical auditorium.[105]

This open theatre was simultaneously grand and intimate; no wonder Shakespeare could be as much at home with public oratory and quiet soliloquy as with conventional dramatic dialogue. The promontory of a stage invited soliloquy and confidential asides, and in that neutral light the relationship of actor and audience was so close as to become a creative collaboration. The spectators could be drawn into the action as participants: when Hamlet makes his dying appeal to those *that are but mutes or audience to this act*, it seems that not only the silent courtiers on the stage but also the spectators in the playhouse are gathering to hear him. On the bare stage the action of a play is unlocalised for much, perhaps most, of the time: where a scene takes place is often unimportant, and the narrative moves freely. Sometimes, indeed, this very absence of localising identity is itself poetically expressive: mad Lear meets blind Gloucester anywhere under the skies.

On the other hand, Shakespeare's plays, at least from *Romeo and Juliet* and *A Midsummer Night's Dream* onwards, also show the skill with which he induces a suspension of disbelief by enriching the narrative with a sense of place, or time, or atmosphere. In the afternoon playhouse the feeling of darkness (or summer, or storm) was created by the words of the poet playing on the responsive imagination of the listener, whether in great set pieces, as when the Chorus describes the *poring dark* of the night before Agincourt, or by the accumulation of brief and passing verbal signals like those which call up the four nights-and-dawns of *Romeo and Juliet*. It was by way of the poet's words that the tiring-house, usually ignored, occasionally became visible again, as, for instance, Macbeth's pleasant castle of Inverness with the temple-haunting martlets nesting in the eaves. The same evocative power turned the empty stage into an orchard or a bedchamber, a foundering ship or a moonlit forest. It was, of course, a usefully flexible method: a busy Roman street becomes, without any break in the dialogue or action, and certainly no change of scenery, the Capitol where Caesar is murdered.

The Elizabethan public playhouse was the home of the poetic drama, and happily there appeared at just the right moment a poet of genius whose chief interest was in writing for the stage. There are clues enough in the plays that Shakespeare was a conscious artist, not working merely by instinct but well aware of what he was doing. The Choruses of *Henry V* identify the creative collaboration by which the words of the poet *work* on the *imaginary forces* of his listeners, while he asks them in return to *work, work* their thoughts. When the Mechanicals in *A Midsummer Night's Dream* prepare their Interlude for the Duke, they grapple with the problems that confronted Shakespeare himself: their consideration of how best to bring moonlight into a chamber is a miniature treatise on dramaturgy. Their first solution is naturalistic – to open a casement so that the real moon may shine in on their performance. They then turn to a symbolist method – an actor with a lantern must present the person of Moonshine. The joke is that both these solutions are absurd, and neither is Shakespeare's own. His method is hinted at elsewhere in this moonlit play. The imagination of the poet is as creative as that of the lunatic or the lover;

but unlike them he does not merely see the unseen – he gives it form in words:

> *And as imagination bodies forth*
> *The forms of things unknown, the poet's pen*
> *Turns them to shapes, and gives to airy nothing*
> *A local habitation and a name.*

It is not surprising that so many of the famously pictorial moments in Shakespeare – the death of Ophelia, the little Princes innocently asleep in the Tower, Cleopatra in her gilded barge – never appear on the stage at all but are given life only in words.

The opening of the Globe in the summer or early autumn of 1599 ushered in a period of astonishing creativity for Shakespeare: he was writing with complete mastery and freedom. Probably the first of his plays to be presented there was *Julius Caesar*:[106] a Swiss tourist, Thomas Platter, saw what was probably one of the earliest performances of the new play in the new playhouse. Shakespeare found his material in *The Lives of the Noble Grecians and Romans*, Sir Thomas North's English version of Plutarch's *Parallel Lives*. In 1595 Richard Field had brought out a new edition of this famous book, which fed Shakespeare's imagination generously – it was the chief source

'On 21 September, after a quick meal, at about two o'clock, I crossed the river with my companions and in a thatched building we saw a performance of the tragedy of Julius, the first of the Caesars. There were about fifteen characters in the play and it was very skilfully done. At the end, as is usual with them, they did a very pretty dance, delightfully combining in pairs, each dressed in either men's or women's clothing ...'

THOMAS PLATTER (1574–1628), TRANSLATED BY JOHN JEREMY

for three of his plays and provided details for several others. The influence of North's Plutarch can be sensed in the diction which contributes so much to the distinctively Roman tone of *Julius Caesar*, grave, plain, formal, understated.

Of course Shakespeare's antique Rome is seen through Elizabethan spectacles. On the stage of the Globe, Burbage and the others were probably costumed in a magnificent hotch-potch of Elizabethan and Roman dress, not unlike figures in a Veronese painting.[107] A drawing of characters from *Titus Andronicus*, attributed to Henry Peacham and probably made in the 1590s, shows just such a mixture of styles. Shakespeare's Caesar wears a *doublet*; Brutus's night visitors are recognisably Elizabethan plotters with conspiratorial *hats* and *cloaks*; the plebeians have *sweaty nightcaps*, and throw them in the air, just as the London crowds customarily did when Queen Elizabeth passed by – London's working-men were bound by statute to wear woollen caps made in England.[108] The crowd of *tag-rag people* on the stage is an extension of the crowd of groundlings in the yard: they *clap* and *hiss* Caesar just as they *do the players in the theatre*.

The Elizabethan colouring of *Julius Caesar* is not just a matter of visual details. In that age of furiously conflicting ideologies, tyrannicide was a much debated topic and a very real possibility. In the autumn of 1598 a certain Edward Squire was arrested for trying to murder the Queen by rubbing poison on her horse's saddle. It was said that he had been suborned by Jesuits, and on 23 November he suffered a traitor's death at Tyburn. While Shakespeare was at work on *Julius Caesar*, pamphleteers were joining battle to debate Squire's case. This is not the only play which raises the issue of whether a subject could ever be justified in ridding the state of a dangerous, or wrong-headed, or feckless ruler. As usual, Shakespeare implies questions and offers no conclusions. Caesar is destroyed because he is dangerous, and to stop him becoming a tyrant; his murder is solemnized as a sort of ritual. But

A drawing of characters from *Titus Andronicus*, showing the mixture of Elizabeth and Roman dress they wore

the assassination is also an outrage against nature and order, and Caesar's *three and thirty wounds* cry for revenge; in the disorder that follows a harmless bystander (who happens to be a poet) is torn to pieces; *domestic fury and fierce civil strife* bring *blood and destruction*; soon *the dogs of war* are unleashed. And the new political reality that emerges out of the chaos is the cynical rule of Antony and Octavius; what was true of Caesar is just as true of them:

> *Th'abuse of greatness is when it disjoins*
> *Remorse from power.*

It was soon after the signing of the Globe lease that Will Kempe left the Company. There may have been some disagreement, and, if so, it is interesting that Kempe, the star comic, departed and Shakespeare the writer remained. Things had changed since Greene lamented the subjection of writers to the pleasure of actors. Kempe's successor as chief clown was Robert Armin (1570?–1615), a writer himself, and probably a singer too. He had learned his craft from Tarlton. He was quite unlike Kempe as a performer, a specialist in the delivery of brilliant and knowing verbal wit. For him Shakespeare invented the Gravedigger, whose *absolute* way with words disconcerts Hamlet, and Feste, the *witty fool* of *Twelfth Night*, who can turn a sentence inside out like a cheveril glove. Perhaps Armin's most extraordinary contribution to Shakespeare's work was in *King Lear*, where the Fool's riddles and jokes and songs, the stock-in-trade of the professional jester, are an essential element in the cruelly developing tragedy. His first important part was probably Touchstone in *As You Like It*, a kind of transitional clown, as if Shakespeare, writing with Kempe still partly in mind, was in danger of falling between two fools. Touchstone is both a *roynish clown* and a professional jester, a *motley fool* whose brain is *as dry as the remainder biscuit after a voyage*.

In writing *As You Like It*,[109] his perfect pastoral comedy, Shakespeare was no doubt influenced by the success of the Admiral's Men in exploiting the fashion for the pastoral with a play about Robin Hood and 'merry Sherwood'. Shakespeare both enjoys and undermines the pastoral convention. His Forest of Arden, where the banished Duke and his followers *live like the old Robin Hood of England*, is not just a pastoral Arcadia: the bitter sky freezes, and the shepherd's hands are greasy from handling the ewes. The idealised love which is part of the convention is both celebrated and mocked – *men have died from time to time, and worms have eaten them, but not for love*. But in spite of its touches of reality, it is an ebullient love-story and one of Shakespeare's happiest plays. The melancholy Jaques, like Touchstone, is Shakespeare's own addition to his source (a romance by Thomas Lodge); but even he does not seriously darken the serenity of the play: his bleakest vision of old age, second childishness and mere oblivion, is belied at the very moment he gives it utterance, by the gallant loyalty of the old servant Adam. There is a tradition, derived, it is said, from the shaky memory of an ancient kinsman, that Shakespeare himself played the part of Adam.

Henslowe and Alleyn responded to the challenge of the Globe by providing the Admiral's Men with a new playhouse too, the Fortune, built as far away as possible from the Globe, north of the city wall, near Finsbury Fields. They were ready to learn from their rivals: the building contract of the Fortune laid down that it should resemble 'the late erected playhouse on the Bank ... called the Globe', and Peter Street was given the job of constructing it. This was not the only change in the theatre world. The Children's Companies were appearing again, and in 1600 the Burbages succeeded in leasing out their Blackfriars playhouse to one of them, the Chapel Children. They were fashionable competition for the adult companies, particularly as they seemed to attract controversial writers; through the mouths of these precocious players Ben Jonson and the brilliant newcomer John Marston (1575?–1634) attacked each other in what became known as the Poetomachia, the War of the Poets. Marston was a significant voice of a younger generation, and his sardonic and unpredictable writing made plays like *Julius Caesar* seem old-fashioned.

But in 1600 – the year in which Morocco the wonder-horse climbed to the top of St Paul's – Shakespeare was doing some exploring of his own: he was writing *Hamlet*.[110] As with the history plays, he both followed and transformed an established theatrical convention. *Hamlet* is a Revenge Play in the tradition of *The Spanish Tragedy*, complete with a vengeful ghost, madness pretended and real, and a fateful play within the play; but to this familiar recipe Shakespeare added the transforming ingredient of his central figure. Hamlet was not the only introspective character on the Elizabethan stage, and not the first in Shakespeare's own work – Richard II and Brutus have their self-questioning soliloquies. But the sense of a preoccupying inner life which Shakespeare created for Hamlet is unlike anything that went before it. His personal questionings shade into wider reflections about what it is to be a human being, *noble in reason* but also the *quintessence of dust*; and they are in tune with Shakespeare's time. In the play's world the old certainties are still powerful – it is still possible to believe that there is *special providence in the fall of a sparrow*; but they coexist with a sceptical, relativist spirit – *there is nothing either good or bad but thinking makes it so.*

While *Julius Caesar* is prevailingly solemn, *Hamlet* is Shakespeare's funniest tragedy; but although the wit is often sardonic it is not explicitly satirical, even when, in the long episode of the Players, Shakespeare topically brings the affairs of theatrical London into the story. He paints an affectionate picture of a city troupe forced to travel by competition from *an eyrie of children* who *berattle the common stages.* In the travelling company are familiar playhouse types, including the dry fool, the man of humours (Jaques, perhaps), and, of course, the lady who is really a boy-player, now growing tall and with a voice soon to be *cracked within the ring.* Shakespeare makes Hamlet sympathetic towards the profession: actors are *the abstracts and brief chronicles of the time*, and their business is an honourable one, to hold the mirror up to nature. Hamlet's preference is for classical restraint of style in both the writing and the acting of plays. The observations about the theatre are appropriate to the refined taste of the fictional prince; they may or may not represent the feelings of Shakespeare himself. His own plays are certainly not restrained; they often require the actor to *tear a passion to tatters*; they contain plenty of the *sallets*, bawdy touches, which Hamlet dislikes but which *make the matter savoury.* Rather than being *caviare to the general* they seem to have had a wide and popular appeal.

Hamlet was certainly popular. In 1607, during the third voyage of the newly formed East India Company, Captain William Keeling anchored his ship, the *Dragon*, off the coast of West Africa, and there his men 'gave the tragedy of *Hamlet*'.[111] The performance of this huge play cannot have displeased the Captain, since a few months later, now on the other side of Africa, he invited Captain

William Hawkins of the *Hector* to a fish dinner and again 'had *Hamlet* acted aboard me: which I permit to keep my people from idleness and unlawful games, or sleep'. His guest Hawkins eventually reached the Mughal city of Agra and became the favoured companion of the Emperor Jahangir, who approved of his ability to speak Turkish. It is irresistible to wonder whether he was fluent enough to entertain that gifted and enquiring potentate with an account of the shipboard *Hamlet*. Jahangir would surely have understood the dysfunctional royal family of Shakespeare's Denmark – his own son had recently tried to assassinate him. And he knew about theatrical effect. An English envoy of the time[112] saw Jahangir set in his court 'like a king in a play, and all the nobles and myself below on a stage covered with carpets – a just theatre'.

Hamlet is usually seen as the first of Shakespeare's great tragedies, *Twelfth Night* as the last of his comedies of lyric love:[113] he had come a long way since *Titus Andronicus* and *The Two Gentlemen of Verona*. The love-plots of *Twelfth Night* depend on an old device which seems to have been a favourite with Elizabethan audiences, a boy-player acting the part of a girl disguised as a boy. Shakespeare had already used this trick in three plays (and was to use it again, in *Cymbeline*). As well as being an excellent source of comedy, this confusion of gender may sometimes have been intended to convey a teasing tone of sexual ambivalence – but then, if the Puritans were to be believed, theatre of any kind tended to deprave and corrupt. According to one moralist, the typical playgoer enjoys the bawdy speeches, the kissing and winking and glancing of wanton eyes, and then makes his way homeward with his chosen companion 'very friendly, and in their secret conclaves (covertly) they play the sodomites, or worse'.[114] However, there is certainly no ambivalence in the disguised Viola: it is from her essential femininity that Shakespeare draws, sometimes simultaneously, both the pathos and the comedy of her situation.

For the romantic elements in his play Shakespeare returned to lyric verse, which he handled with new artistry – Viola's most famous lines are so poignantly beautiful that Joseph Haydn was drawn to set them to music. The farcical plot is a distorting mirror for the romance, and it is Shakespeare at his most extravagant and inventive, so hectically absurd that he actually challenges the disbelief of the audience: *If this were played upon a stage now, I could condemn it as an improbable fiction.* Malvolio, the Puritan who is really a secret sensualist, was bound to be a hit in the playhouse, and he at once became as popular a stage figure as Hamlet: when in February 1602 the lawyer John Manningham saw the play at the Middle Temple, it was the tricking of Malvolio he chiefly remembered.

There are touches of autumnal melancholy too, especially in the Fool's songs. Shakespeare's plays often call for music, but in both *As You Like It* and *Twelfth Night* there are more songs than usual, finely woven into the dramatic texture. Shakespeare's interest may have been stimulated by Armin's skill as a singer, but he was also responding to the changing culture of his time: the English lute-song was beginning its brief and glorious flowering – it lasted for perhaps 25 years. The greatest of the lutenists, John Dowland (1563?–1626) brought out his *First Book of Songs or Airs* in 1597; in 1600 there followed *The First Book of Airs or Little Short Songs* by Thomas Morley (1557?–1602), which included a setting, the earliest known, of the song of the two pages in *As You Like It*. The roisterers in *Twelfth Night* sing snatches from yet another collection published in 1600, Robert Jones's airs 'which may be sung to the lute, orpharian or viol de gambo' (Sir Andrew Aguecheek *plays o'th'viol-de-gamboys*).

Shakespeare and Morley must have known each other. They

were neighbours near Bishopsgate when Morley was working on his influential book *A Plain and Easy Introduction to Practical Music*; in it he insists that the composer of a song must always respect the words so that there is 'a perfect agreement and, as it were, an harmonical consent betwixt the matter and the music'. Shakespeare would have agreed about this harmonical consent: he was clearly sensitive to the dramatic effect not only of a song's words, but also of its music, like the *sleepy tune* of the unknown song Lucius sings for Brutus, and the *divine air* of Balthasar's song for the hidden Benedick. Before Viola even hears the words of Feste's song it is the tune itself which goes to her heart:

It gives a very echo to the seat
Where love is throned.[115]

The new century brought a beginning and an ending for the family in Stratford. Shakespeare's only sister, Joan, now married to a hatter named William Hart, presented John and Mary Shakespeare with a new grandchild; like both his father and his famous uncle he was given the name of William. Just a year later, John Shakespeare died: he was buried on 8 September 1601. Hamlet gives his father a noble epitaph:

He was a man. Take him for all in all,
I shall not look upon his like again.

Shakespeare's own feelings are hidden. A few months after his father's death he laid out £320 'of current English money' to buy more than a hundred acres of farming land in Old Stratford from the MP William Combe and his nephew John. He seems to have known the Combes well: John was a successful money-lender and said to be the richest man in the town, and he was later to remember Shakespeare in his will. Soon after the Old Stratford

Elizabeth I's favourite the Earl of Essex (1566–1601)

investment, Shakespeare bought a cottage and garden on the other side of the lane which led past New Place; he probably intended it as accommodation for a servant. He was now a man of substantial property, as well as head of the family and a gentleman by inheritance.

In London things were less comfortable. Shortly before John Shakespeare died, the Chamberlain's Men found themselves dangerously entangled in one of the great crises of the reign. Essex's Irish campaign (hopefully celebrated in *Henry V*) turned out a humiliating failure, and when Essex returned to England in 1599 (exactly a week after Thomas Platter visited the Globe), he was committed to house arrest. For 18 months he raged and hoped, tormented by factious jealousy and uncontrollable debts; he complained to the Queen that he was libelled by every 'prating tavern-haunter ... shortly they will play me upon the stage'.[116] In 1601 his frustration broke into rebellion. A group of his followers, including Southampton, worked out a plan to raise London, seize Whitehall and force the Queen to accept their terms. On 7 February, a Saturday, 'they went all together to the Globe over the water', where they had engaged Shakespeare's Company to present *Richard II*, its story of rebellion and deposition making a suitably inflammatory prologue to their own rising. But next day the parade of rebels through the city failed to raise support, and Essex, finding Ludgate barred against him, returned by water to his house in the Strand, where he was arrested. On 25 February he and five of his followers were executed. Southampton escaped relatively lightly – he was sent to the Tower, where, it was said, his black and white cat crept down the chimney to keep him company.

The Chamberlain's Men were lucky to avoid punishment. Under examination, Augustine Phillips, speaking for the Company, claimed that they had been reluctant to present this old story 'of the deposing and killing of King Richard', but they had been offered a higher payment than usual. The Queen certainly understood what was implied by this performance of Shakespeare's play, and it was still in her mind months later. Discussing history with her Keeper of the Records, 'good and honest' William Lambarde, she declared, 'I am Richard II, know ye not that?'

Before his fall Essex had been, at least for his many admirers, England's hero. When George Chapman (1559?–1634) published the first instalment of his translation of Homer it carried a dedication to 'the most honoured now living instance of the Achillean virtues eternized by divine Homer, the Earl of Essex'. Homer's epic of the siege of Troy, together with the medieval addition of the Troilus love-plot, was popular material for Elizabethan poets, and hints in several plays suggest that it had been in Shakespeare's mind for some time. *Troilus and Cressida*[117] is a magnificently cynical treatment, anti-romantic and anti-heroic – Essex would certainly not have enjoyed comparison with Shakespeare's arrogant and treacherous Achilles. The war is presented as bloody and pointless; as the observer Thersites puts it, *All the argument is a whore and a cuckold*. He is perhaps the most scabrous character in Shakespeare, and his sour comments present all the familiar Greek heroes as flawed: Agamemnon *has not so much brain as ear-wax*; Ajax is *sodden-witted*; Ulysses is a *dog-fox* and Nestor *a stale old mouse-eaten dry cheese*; Achilles himself is taken up with his *masculine whore*.

Spectators who expected an epic or a love-story were given a cerebral play: much of the dramatic energy arises out of debate and the interplay of ideas. The diction is startling, the vocabulary remarkable for its erudite distortions of familiar words – *oppugnancy, neglection, propension, rejoindure, recordation, deceptious, orifex*, and many more. The play itself is a puzzle. It may have been intended for a private or learned audience, but according to the title-page of the Quarto it had been acted at the Globe; and yet a later issue of the same edition declared in an *Epistle* to the reader that it had never been 'staled with the stage' or 'sullied with the smoky breath of the multitude'. It is not a restrained play; it is full of adventurous writing; but it has, perhaps, a flavour of Hamlet's caviare to the general. The same Quarto *Epistle* described it as a comedy full of the 'savoured salt of wit', but it is usually classified as a tragedy; in our own time it is often included in the group known as the Problem Plays.

It suited the disillusioned mood of the reign's closing years. In January 1603 the Queen left Whitehall for Richmond Palace, her 'warm winter box' with its south-facing chambers hung with arras and overlooking pleasant gardens.[118] The Chamberlain's Men played before her for the last time during the Candlemas Revel at the beginning of February. She told her godson that she felt creeping time at the gate; it soon became clear that her capricious vitality was failing. On 19 March the playhouses were silenced. She died five days later, giving at last a gesture of assent that her cousin, James VI of Scotland, should succeed her as James I of England. It might be thought proper for the kingdom's poets to turn out verses of mourning, but, as Henry Chettle ornately and reproachfully put it in his own elegy, Shakespeare did not 'drop from his honeyed muse one sable tear'.[119]

Rare new liveries 1603–05

The new reign at once brought a gratifying change for Shake-speare and the players: within days of his arrival in London, King James took into his own hands the patronage of the Chamber-lain's Men. They were now the King's Men, licensed to exercise their art and faculty of playing, not only in their 'now usual house called the Globe', but also, without lets, hindrances or molesta-tions, at any convenient place throughout the kingdom. In theory it would not be possible any longer for a Puritan corporation to make difficulties (the reality did not always follow – in Stratford plays were already banned from the town, and in 1611 the fine for licensing a performance would be raised from ten shillings to £10). The principal men of the Company were named in the royal patent: first on the list was Lawrence Fletcher, an actor who had been favoured by the King in Scotland, but who probably never worked at the Globe; Shakespeare's name headed the rest. Some months passed before the other London companies were granted royal patronage too: the Admiral's became Prince Henry's Men, Worcester's became Queen Anne's Men, and the Chapel Children were to be known as the Children of the Queen's Revels.

However, at this promising moment the playhouses were actually closed. In the spring of 1603 the players' old enemy, the plague, which had held off for several years, crept back into London, and the infection quickly spread to become the third really serious outbreak of Shakespeare's lifetime. More than 30,000 people died, among them Ben Jonson's small son. His grief at this loss was very different from Shakespeare's silence at the death of Hamnet. It was in a vision, Jonson said, that he learned that the child had died, and he addressed his 'lov'd boy' in a moving short poem, *On My First Son*:

'Rest in soft peace, and, ask'd, say here doth lie
Ben Jonson his best piece of poetry.'

The King's Men went on their travels, fetching up in Mortlake, where Augustine Phillips had a house. In London on the day of the coronation, 25 July, the streets were thronged with people defying the infection, and the river was crowded with boats; but the ceremony itself was a subdued affair and prudently admission tickets were required.[120] The great London celebration planned for the new monarch had to be postponed. Immediately after the coronation, James moved to Hampton Court, and soon after began a long and enjoyable progress through the southern part of his kingdom. He stayed for a while at Wilton, the great house which the Countess of Pembroke, 'a second Minerva',[121] had turned into a haven for poets, and there he was entertained by his own Company: the King's Men made the journey from Mortlake and, on 2 December, acted for the first time before their new patron. They were well rewarded with £30 for their 'pains and expenses', and they were soon in

'At that time the pest was in London, he being in the country ... he saw in a vision his eldest son (then a child and at London) appear unto him with the mark of a bloody cross on his forehead as if it had been cutted with a sword ... In the mean time comes there letters from his wife of the death of that boy in the plague. He appeared to him, he said, of a manly shape and of that growth that he thinks he shall be at the resurrection.'

WILLIAM DRUMMOND OF HAWTHORNDEN, *CERTAIN INFORMATIONS AND MANNERS OF BEN JONSON* (1619)

demand again: during that winter's Revels, held at Hampton Court, they presented no less than six plays. In February they received another £30, 'by way of His Majesty's free gift', for their relief while the plague prevented them from working in London. Things had certainly changed for Shakespeare and his friends in the Company.

In fact the plague was already beginning to relent, and in March London was at last able to stage its celebration. It was a tremendous affair, a royal procession from the Tower to Whitehall by way of seven triumphal arches rich with allegory. Typical of them was the 40-foot high Arch of London, at the beginning of the processional route. As the King approached, a silken curtain 'painted like a thick cloud' swept aside to reveal, at the top of the arch, a panorama of London, 'adorned with houses, towers and steeples, set off in perspective'. In one of the niches below reclined a figure representing the Thames, 'in a skin-coat made like flesh, naked, and blue'. And in the central alcove stood Edward Alleyn as the Genius of the City, with mantle and buskins of purple and a crown of plane-leaves on his white wig. 'With excellent action, and a well-tuned audible voice', he pronounced Jonson's welcoming address to 'greatest James, and no less good than great'. Meanwhile the conduits of the city 'ran claret wine very plenteously'.[122] The King was attended by city notables, prelates, courtiers, noblemen – among them Southampton, now restored to royal favour.

Although Shakespeare and the King's Men are not on record as having walked in the procession, it was certainly a ceremonial day for them. To mark the occasion, the Master of the Wardrobe presented nine members of the Company (Shakespeare's name headed the list) with four and a half yards of red cloth each, so that they could wear the King's livery. It was not a particularly lavish gift, and they were not singled out by it: all sorts of attendants and functionaries, including members of the other players' companies, received the same treatment. But it was an identifiable mark of

King James I (1566–1625)

status: Shakespeare was now a Groom of the Chamber, a member of the royal household. He and his friends soon found themselves serving the King in a way that had little to do with the theatre. Negotiations for peace with Spain, a matter close to James's heart, were taking place that summer, and for the better part of August the principal men of the Company were required to attend on the Spanish envoy, the Constable of Castile, in Somerset House. At the same time ten of Queen Anne's Men were at Durham House, attendant on the Flemish Count of Aremberg.

Shakespeare was no longer a young man with his way to make. In April he had turned 40, the time which was thought to begin 'the first part of the old man's age',[123] and he was the leading member of the company most favoured at court. The Queen, Anne of Denmark, loved plays, and although the King was sometimes bored by them, it mattered to him that his court should be magnificent, more so even than his predecessor's; lavish entertainments were part of that magnificence. During his reign there were many more performances of plays at court than in the days of Elizabeth, and the King's Men gave more of them than the other companies put together. Between the beginning of November in 1604 and the beginning of Lent in February 1605 they were called on a dozen times. *The Merchant of Venice*, which they gave on 10 February, must have been a particular success, since two days later it was presented again 'by the King's command'.

Among the plays given at court that Christmas was *Measure for Measure*.[124] Its first line seems to promise a play of ideas to raise the censor's hackles: *Of government the properties to unfold* … It might be thought a risky way to greet a new monarch. King James, while he was still in his teens, had written a *Short Treatise*[125] of advice to Scottish poets, and among its routine observations on style and subject-matter, one passage has the ring of personal conviction: 'You must also beware of writing anything of matters of common weal ... they are too grave matters for a poet to mell in.' But Shakespeare did not court controversy; his focus is not political. The title, more helpful than usual, is derived from the Sermon on the Mount in St Matthew's Gospel: 'Judge not that ye be not judged ... with that measure ye mete, it shall be measured to you again.' The great and opposed concerns of just government, *mortality* and *mercy* ... *terror* and *love*, broaden into a consideration of man's moral nature.

The play is a daring mixture of tones. Shakespeare derived the plot from an Italian story, by way of an English play,[126] and its ingredients – the corrupt judge and the maiden sore beset – are reminiscent of folklore or popular romance, as are the clever tricks by which the plot is disentangled. The Duke walking incognito among his people is a figure from an old tale; but, as Shakespeare's own addition to the story, he has a special complexity: it is one of longest and most puzzling parts he ever wrote. The amiable lyric tone proper to romance, however, is almost entirely absent, and much of the diction is concentrated and intellectual: difficulties and oddities in Shakespeare's dramatic language, already evident in *Troilus*, are becoming more marked. The most intense scenes are two complex confrontational debates.

Earth-bound comic episodes provide a jolly commentary on the main plot. The Vienna of the play, where the Duke sees *corruption boil and bubble*, is Shakespeare's London; the sex-trade, as on Bankside, is vigorously active in spite of *the war* and *the sweat* and *the gallows*. The bawd Pompey, whose bum is the greatest thing about him, offers a cheerfully pragmatic view of morality: sin cannot be legislated out of existence; unless the authorities *mean to geld and spay all the youth of the city* fallible human beings *will to't*, as always. The main plot provides its own kind of moral sympathy in a situation which seems to demand moral rigour:

They say best men are moulded out of faults
And, for the most, become much more the better
For being a little bad.

Another new play seen at court in 1604 was *Othello, The Moor of Venice*.[127] Its plot came, like that of *Measure for Measure*, from a story by Giraldi Cinthio, and the way in which Shakespeare transformed it shows the completeness of his control. The chief instrument of this transformation is, of course, the language, but there are structural and narrative changes too. Shakespeare manipulates fictional time with virtuosity, compressing Cinthio's indeterminate time-scheme so that the destruction of Othello takes a single devastating day; and yet, in a kind of parallel time, the audience is led by the nose to feel days or weeks have passed. Another crucial change is the tragic ending Shakespeare invented for the play. In Cinthio's brutal tale, the Moor does not kill his wife himself, but orders the Ensign (the Iago figure) to do the job: he bludgeons the lady to death with a sand-filled stocking and pulls the rafters down upon her to conceal the crime. Cinthio's ensign has a clear and simple motive for his villainy. Shakespeare's Iago, on the other hand, is a famous puzzle, his confused and contradictory motives forming part of the mysterious power of the play. He develops his design like a creative artist (*'Tis here, but yet confused ...*), and it is with aesthetic pleasure that he watches his poison *burn like the mines of sulphur*.

Othello was not the only black man in the drama of the time ('black' was as imprecise a descriptive term then as it is now): Shakespeare himself had twice before brought a Moor on to the stage. There are few specific references to Othello's colour in the play – it is spoken of coarsely by Iago, furiously by Brabantio, despairingly by Othello himself, but otherwise largely ignored; and he certainly does not meet with the sort of hatred or contempt that Shylock suffers among the Venetians. Nevertheless in performance on the stage his colour is always there, a visible token of difference; and this difference, this strangeness, which sets Othello apart from the super-subtle Venetian, is at the core of the tragedy.

Black people were certainly not unknown in Shakespeare's England.[128] Indeed there was a black trumpeter, facetiously known as John Blank, at the court of Henry VIII.[129] But it was during the 1550s that numbers began to increase noticeably. It became fashionable to keep a blackamoor servant, and things Moorish could seem attractively exotic: Shakespeare's Prince of Morocco, *a tawny Moor all in white*, is a glamorous figure. For the Twelfth Night Revel of 1605 Ben Jonson and Inigo Jones collaborated on a *Masque of Blackness*, in which the Queen and her ladies appeared as the Daughters of Niger, with their arms and faces painted black, their hair 'thick and curled upright', and at ear, neck and wrist ornaments of orient pearls, 'best setting off from black'. But even in the prettified context of the masque blackness was not being presented as in any real sense beautiful or acceptable: Jonson's nymphs, it turns out, are travelling to Britain, where the sun 'will blanch an Ethiop' and they will find their beauties 'scorched no more'.

In the real world outside the masque reactions at court or in the street were even less sympathetic: a Moorish embassy to London in 1600 was treated shabbily by Elizabethan standards. If immigrants from Europe often had a hard time of it, for black immigrants things could be worse still. In a letter of 1596 to the Lord Mayor and other civic leaders, the Queen announced that there were too many blackamoors now in her realm and that 'those kind of people' should be sent away; a Proclamation of 1601 declared that 'the great number of negroes and blackamoors' was taking relief away from the native English.

Shakespeare was not above the occasional gibe at foreigners – at the subtle-witted French, the drunken Dane, the swag-bellied Hollander, to say nothing of the weasel Scot, the Irishman of the bogs and the Welshman whose speech makes fritters of English. But he could also write with understanding about the foreigners in London. At some time during the 1590s a play of *Sir Thomas More* ran into trouble with the censor and was put into cold storage; it was not brought out again until the beginning of the new reign, when several writers collaborated to revise it; Shakespeare is generally believed to have been one of them. The longer of the two passages thought to be by him treats of this matter of the foreign presence in London – and it is of extraordinary, though incidental, interest as the only known example, other than a few signatures, of his handwriting: it seems to be the work of a fast and confident writer who seldom troubles with punctuation, corrects as he writes, and makes use of time-saving contractions like *pvince* for 'province' and *matie* for 'majesty'.

This longer passage is about the disturbances of 'Evil May Day' in 1517, when Thomas More, as Sheriff of London, confronted violent rioters demanding the expulsion of foreigners from the city. Their complaints are familiar: the foreigners drive up prices, they *eat more in our country than they do in their own*, they spread infection, they damage the trade of poor craftsmen. In his fine rebuke of the rioters, More demands that they search in themselves for understanding of what the refugees suffer:

> *Imagine that you see the wretched strangers,*
> *Their babies at their backs, with their poor luggage*
> *Plodding to th'ports and coasts for transportation …*

Suppose the rioters found themselves forced to take refuge in France or Flanders and met there only the *mountainish inhumanity* they themselves had shown; what would they feel then?

Shakespeare knew London immigrants; indeed, by 1604 he was lodging in an immigrant household. He had left Bankside and moved across the river to a well-to-do neighbourhood near

Cripplegate; down the road lived John Heminges, and the book-sellers of St Paul's were not very far away. Shakespeare's lodging was in Silver Street, in the house of a certain Christopher Mountjoy, a French Huguenot who had set up in business as a maker of head-dresses for grand ladies. Shakespeare and the family got on well: Mountjoy's wife asked for his help in arranging a marriage between her daughter and a former apprentice of theirs, Stephen Belott – his mother was French too. Shakespeare obliged and the marriage duly took place, but unfortunately it did not last: Belott and Mountjoy fell out over the honouring of the marriage settlement Shakespeare had helped to arrange. In 1612 the dispute came to court, and Shakespeare, probably living by then in Stratford, was called to testify. From the cloudy language of the reported depositions he emerges as amiable and a little vague: he had known both parties for ten years 'or thereabouts'; he remembered Belott as 'a very good and industrious servant', remembered too that Mountjoy had shown Belott 'great good will and affection'; there had certainly been promises of money and goods, but he could not recall the precise sums and did not know 'what implements and necessaries of household stuff' had been involved. Perhaps after a gap of eight years his memory really was hazy – or perhaps he simply did not wish to be caught up in what had become a disreputable family quarrel: the elders of the French church in London considered both Mountjoy and his son-in-law to be dissolute persons.[130]

Given the events in Silver Street, the title of the play Shakespeare probably wrote while he was lodging there has an ironic ring: *All's Well That Ends Well*.[131] It is a curious play, experimental in feeling, a love story in which Shakespeare changes, or inverts, the usual patterns. It begins, rather than ends, with a marriage, and it is the lady who drives the events, pursuing a reluctant husband until he is at last brought to promise that he will *love her dearly, ever ever dearly*. The plot comes from one of Boccaccio's tales, and, by creating formidable social and moral differences between the heroine, Helen (or Helena), and her husband, Bertram, Shakespeare transforms a neat story into a celebration of love which is beyond explanation or commonsense. Helen, a poor physician's daughter, is selfless, resourceful, and lovable too – *the sweet marjoram of the salad, or rather the herb of grace*. Her love is irrational and inexhaustible:

> *I know I love in vain, strive against love;*
> *Yet in this captious and intenable sieve*
> *I still pour in the waters of my love ...*

Her husband, on the other hand, is a nobleman, and also shallow, false, *a foolish idle boy, but for all that very ruttish* (not surprisingly, commentators have spied in Bertram, with *his arched brows, his hawking eye, his curls*, a hint of the young man of the Sonnets).

Shakespeare seems to have enjoyed depicting baffled fathers of wayward daughters – Egeus, Capulet, Brabantio; in this play he has a mother with a refractory son. The Countess, wise, affectionate and exasperated, is Shakespeare's addition to the Boccaccio plot, and her presence contributes to the warmly tolerant tone of the play. *All's Well* has not supplied the world with many quotations – its language is not obviously decorative, but spare, sometimes difficult, often surprising. But one well-known passage aptly evokes the play's generous spirit: *The web of our life is of a mingled yarn, good and ill together. Our virtues would be proud if our faults whipped them not, and our crimes would despair if they were not cherished by our virtues.*

It may well have been near this time that Shakespeare was working on an even more curious play, *Timon of Athens*[132] – it is impossible to know for certain when it was written, and it is something of a puzzle in other ways too. The Folio text is very confused, so much so that some scholars have judged the play to be unfinished, with several sections only roughed out. It has been suggested that Shakespeare was not fully committed to his own play.[133] Other scholars have argued, perhaps more persuasively, that the play shows signs of uneasy collaboration, that Shakespeare was not the sole author, and that his collaborator may have been the young and gifted Thomas Middleton (1580–1627). Whatever the explanation, *Timon* is certainly unlike any of the other plays. The plot is extraordinarily simple and pared down; the persons of the play have almost no individuality, and some are not even given names; the part of Timon, though intense, is without complexity – he even sees himself as an archetype: *I am Misanthropos, and hate mankind.*

However, it is certainly not a dull play. The dramatic energy is generated not by the narrative but by the tone, the savagery conveyed in the escalation of Timon's hatred, as his rage at the ingratitude of Athens and the Athenian sycophants grows into universal loathing – of sons, limping sires, dimpled babes, whores, usurers, physicians, lawyers, even the moon and the sun and the earth that engenders arrogant man along with the black toad and eyeless venomed worm. His huge curses call down plague, cold sciatica, itches, blains, general leprosy and consumptions in the hollow bones of men; he invokes *contumelious, beastly, mad-brained war*, and the destruction of piety, peace, truth, domestic awe, night rest, and all degrees, customs and laws. Only towards the close of the play are there moments of quietness as he welcomes the end of the *long sickness* of his life and contemplates his gravestone washed by *the light foam of the sea*.

Naturally commentators have been tempted to think that while Shakespeare was writing *Timon* he must have been fighting some personal demon of his own. The great scholar Sir Edmund Chambers offers, admitting that it is a subjective view, the suggestion that Shakespeare might have been close to some kind of breakdown.[134] It is certainly puzzling that, just as he was about to reach the highest point of his powers, he should actually choose to write a play as strange as this; but for the assurance with which he conveys manic misanthropy no explanation of inner demons is needed: the imaginative empathy that could create both Isabella and Iago could certainly also create the crazy sufferings of Timon.

At any rate, the real Shakespeare does not seem to have shared the fictional Timon's loathing of wealth, the *common whore of mankind*; in matters financial there was no hint of a breakdown. In 1604 he took a Stratford apothecary named Philip Rogers to court in order to recover a debt of rather under £2; in 1608 he pursued a certain John Addenbrooke in the same way. At the time when he was about to write *King Lear*, with its great prayer for *poor naked wretches* everywhere, he was carefully organising his own finances. In 1605 he laid out the very large sum of £440 for a part-interest in the lease of certain Stratford tithes. By this time, tithes, once a levy paid to the Church, had come to be a form of corporation tax: in return for this lump sum and an annual fee to the Corporation, Shakespeare bought the right to administer the collection of these taxes himself. He expected to benefit by a useful £60 a year.

Great power, great transcendence 1605–08

Between 1605 and 1608 Shakespeare wrote four incomparable tragedies – and also tried his hand at a new kind of tragi-comedy. *King Lear*,[135] the first of these tragedies, offers some of the clearest insights into the artistry with which he handled his source-material. Several different sources contributed to this great play (Holinshed, Spenser's *The Faerie Queene*, Sidney's *Arcadia*, an old chronicle play of *King Leir*), but the most eccentric was a brilliant and unpleasant propagandist pamphlet published in 1603 and entitled *A Declaration of Egregious Popish Impostures*. The writer was Samuel Harsnett (1561–1613), a cleric well on his way up ambition's ladder – he would eventually become Archbishop of York and a Privy Councillor. His book is an account of the exorcisms by which, it was said, Popish priests drew converts during the 1580s, and Shakespeare may have had a personal reason for dipping into it: one of the priests in question was Robert Debdale from Anne Shakespeare's home village of Shottery.[136] Nightmare anecdotal details drawn from Harsnett contributed to the play's sense of irrational and authoritarian cruelty.

Shakespeare's own additions to the story are crucial. Among them is the Fool; and it is hardly fanciful to imagine him gathering ideas from Armin as he worked on that ambiguous character with his tormenting riddles and fragmentary songs. The madness in the play is also Shakespeare's invention – both *the great rage* to which Lear is driven by his *pelican daughters*, and the pretended madness of Edgar in his disguise as a Bedlam beggar, *whipped from tithing to tithing* and reduced to swallowing *the old rat and the ditch-dog*. The long storm sequence is also Shakespeare's own, and it is a striking example of his poetic drama at work. Within a naturalistic theatrical convention, 'the contemptible machinery by which they mimic the storm'[137] inevitably seems inadequate. Shakespeare's storm was designed for the bare and daylit Globe, and, writing at full stretch, he was able through the power of poetry to evoke several storms at once: the physical drenching that makes it *a naughty night to swim in*; the tempest in Lear's mind which drives away all feeling else; the universal disorder he invokes:

> *Strike flat the thick rotundity o'th'world,*
> *Crack nature's moulds, all germens spill at once*
> *That makes ingrateful man.*

Shakespeare actually makes his method of the poetic drama part of the story. When Edgar tricks his blind father into thinking that he is at the *extreme verge* of a dizzying cliff, it is with words that he creates his illusion; at that moment he is a poet-dramatist working on his father's imagination. He succeeds: it is from a cliff of the imagination that Gloucester falls to the bare boards of the stage. It is not surprising that for a time the play was thought too wild to present without alteration. When Nahum Tate (1652–1715) rewrote it to suit the theatrical taste of the time, he described it as 'a heap of jewels, unstrung and unpolished ... dazzling in their disorder'. Harsnett, who knew a good deal about the theatre, subscribed to the traditional view that the purpose of tragedy 'is moving of affection and passion in the spectators'. It would be interesting to know how much moving of passion went on among the spectators when the King's Men presented *Lear* at court on 26 December 1606. It was the feast of Stephen, the saint invoked in prayer for 'all our sufferings here upon earth'.

Shakespeare was writing *King Lear* and *Macbeth*[138] during the period of the Gunpowder Plot to destroy King and Parliament. For some time before it came to light in November 1605 the Plot had been simmering. There had been a growing sense of frustration among English Catholics. The new King had seemed to promise a better deal for them, and peace with Spain removed a serious difficulty; perhaps the Queen herself had Catholic inclinations – at her coronation she had openly refused Protestant communion. But early in 1605 James, irritated by conflicting demands, announced to his Council that the laws against both Catholics and Puritans would be more strictly enforced; he uncompromisingly declared his utter detestation of Popery. And of course religious frustration was complicated by other resentments, political, factious, economic: some of the conspirators, debt-burdened gentry, had been followers of Essex in his abortive rebellion.

Nahum Tate rewrote *King Lear* for the stage in 1681. His aim was 'to rectify what was wanting in the Regularity and Probability of the tale', and to that end he invented 'a love betwixt Edgar and Cordelia'. At the happy conclusion, the lovers ascend the throne together, while Lear, Gloucester and Kent retire to 'some cool cell' to pass their time in 'calm reflections'. He omitted the Fool altogether. Tate's *Lear* was the only version of the play seen on the London stage for over a century.

As at the time of the Essex rebellion, Shakespeare is just visible on the edge of the main event. Among the London taverns favoured by the conspirators was the Mermaid, where they must have mixed with playhouse folk. Moreover, the Plot had a strong Midlands connection; in particular, the countryside round Stratford was friendly ground. Robert Catesby, the most famous of the plotters, was born at Lapworth, a little to the north of the town, and his father had sheltered Campion there; the house now belonged to another conspirator, Jack Wright. Another, John Grant, lived near Snitterfield, where Richard Shakespeare had worked land. An important centre of conspiracy was Clopton House, which had land touching Shakespeare's own property. The house had been rented by yet another conspirator, Ambrose Rookwood (who was to leave his name boldly cut in the wall of his prison in the Tower). After the discovery of the Plot it was the Bailiff of Stratford who sent men to seize Rookwood's goods: in a cellar at Clopton they found crucifixes, chalices, rosaries and other dangerous things.

The fear of terrorism persisted for months. The crackdown on Catholic dissent, which had begun before the Plot, became more severe after it. Discreet evasion of the sacraments was no longer acceptable. In May 1606 21 people were summoned before the Stratford ecclesiastical court, charged with failure to receive the Easter sacrament; among them were Shakespeare's daughter Susanna and his old friends Hamnet and Judith Sadler. The charge against them was eventually dismissed; the penalty would have been a fine of £20 – rising, for a third offence, to £60, the amount of a whole year's return on Shakespeare's investment in tithes.

For the material of *Macbeth*, as for *King Lear*, Shakespeare relied on Holinshed. The story of a King murdered, of secret treachery and bloody violence, must have seemed frighteningly apposite in the panic of the Plot and the subsequent interrogations and trials. It is not surprising that the play is darkened by

Dire combustion and confused events
New-hatched to th' woeful time.

It may well have been one of the plays presented at Hampton Court or Greenwich in 1606 to celebrate the state visit of the Queen's brother, Christian IV of Denmark; in spite of its dangerous subject and ferocious power, it was apt for presentation at court. As well as being set in the King's home country of Scotland[139] it touched on some of his favourite concerns, his pride in his descent from a line of kings, his views on the nature of kingship and *the king-becoming graces*, his well-known interest in witchcraft. Even the unusual shortness of the play[140] may have reflected his taste: he sometimes showed his boredom openly – he fell asleep during a play at Oxford.

But of course *Macbeth*, written in the full blaze of Shakespeare's powers, is not just an occasional piece. Compliments to James and echoes of the Plot serve the play's larger purposes. For instance, the little description of the *most pious* King Edward the Confessor and his skill in curing people *strangely visited* with scrofula, the King's Evil, was certainly intended to flatter James, who had reluctantly reconciled himself to the ritual of the Royal Touch; but it is also part of the play's cumulative imagery of sickness, Lady Macbeth's *mind diseased*, Macduff's longing for *wholesome days*, the true king's triumphant arrival as *the medicine of the sickly weal*. Similarly it is not just to exploit the topicality of the Gunpowder Plot that Shakespeare touches on Equivocation, the doctrine that a man under hostile interrogation might justifiably evade or twist the truth – a sensational element in the trial, in March 1606, of the Jesuit Henry Garnet. Shakespeare's highly topical references to it are part of a pervasive pattern of ideas in the play: deception and self-deception, moral ambiguity, the slipperiness of truth, which can itself be a weapon of evil: *The instruments of darkness tell us truths.*

Not the least potent element in the atmosphere of unnatural disorder is the sense of darkness called up by the poetry. It is hinted at right at the beginning, in the *fog and filthy air* of the witches, and it gathers gradually with the invocations of Macbeth (*Stars, hide your fires*) and Lady Macbeth (*Come, thick night*), through the torchlit evening of Duncan's arrival, until *the moon is down* and starless night (heaven's *candles are all out*) settles into the playhouse. The night of the murder is prolonged into an unnatural darkness that strangles the sun and entombs the face of earth *when living light should kiss it.* The scheme of *Macbeth* is a single long darkness (*Light thickens* again for the death of Banquo) which does not begin to lift until Malcolm offers his supporters a little comfort:

Receive what cheer you may:
The night is long that never finds the day.

Macbeth is Shakespeare's greatest exploration of evil, but while asserting morality he does not moralize; instead the play compels sympathy for even unrepentant wickedness, which brings its own tragedies: doubt, rage, loneliness and the despairing sense that *what's done cannot be undone.*

In June 1607 Susanna Shakespeare married John Hall, a distinguished physician, though not formally licensed: the College of Physicians, rigorous in London, was tolerant about country practitioners. Hall became an eminent man. His meticulous notes were published after his death, among them a record of treating his daughter's sore neck with 'Aqua Vitae, in which was infused nutmegs, cinnamon, cloves, pepper'. His most often quoted specific was for Michael Drayton's quotidian fever: an emetic infusion mixed with syrup of violets, which 'wrought very well both upwards and downwards'. Despite the fact that he was a godly Puritan and Susanna had Catholic connections, it seems to have been a happy marriage; Shakespeare was certainly on good terms with his son-in-law. In February 1608 a daughter, Elizabeth, was born. When she died in 1670 she was Shakespeare's last direct descendant – she had had two husbands but no children of her own.

However, there may have been, unofficially, another direct descendant, her almost exact contemporary. Sir William Davenant (1606–68) was one of the bright spirits of his time, a theatrical entrepreneur, dramatist and poet who succeeded Ben Jonson as Laureate, and, according to his collaborator John Dryden, 'a man of quick and piercing imagination'. He claimed to be, and probably was, Shakespeare's godson; and over a glass of wine with his intimate friends he would go further and let it be known that he was actually the illegitimate son of the great man. The claim is not implausible. His parents, John and Jane Davenant, kept a tavern in Oxford where, according to Aubrey, Shakespeare 'did commonly in his journey lie' as he travelled between London and Stratford. Jane, Aubrey reports, was 'a very beautiful woman and of a very good wit, and of conversation extremely agreeable'. At the time of Elizabeth Hall's birth, William Davenant was a toddler nearly two years old: he was born in March 1606. If he really was Shakespeare's natural son, an elementary calculation suggests that Shakespeare must have been in Oxford during the summer of 1605 – in time, perhaps, to witness the King's visit to the city and the little show of welcome at the gate of St John's College, when three actors, dressed as sybils, all-hailed him as the descendant of Banquo.

'I was at his funeral. He had a coffin of walnut-tree; Sir John Denham said 'twas the finest coffin that ever he saw. His body was carried in a hearse to Westminster Abbey ... to his grave, which is in the south cross aisle, on which, on a paving stone of marble is writ, in imitation of that on Ben Jonson: *O rare Sir Will. Davenant*. But me thought it had been proper a laurel should have been set on his coffin – which was not done.'

JOHN AUBREY,
LIFE OF SIR WILLIAM DAVENANT

Whatever the truth of Davenant's parentage, he certainly has a place in the Shakespeare story. He was probably the most important link between the Shakespearean playhouses and the very different theatre of the Restoration, and his veneration of his godfather was a vital element in the beginnings of the cult of Shakespeare. He believed that 'he writ with the very spirit that did Shakespeare'; but he also believed, of course, that the plays needed improvement to suit a more refined age. Adaptation was, after all, a kind of compliment: this, with a touch of authorial vanity, is the message of the Prologue to the Dryden-Davenant version of *The Tempest*:

'So, from old Shakespeare's honoured dust, this day
Springs up and buds a new reviving Play.'

For his last two tragedies Shakespeare returned to North's Plutarch. *Antony and Cleopatra*,[141] a huge drama of public action on a grand scale, could scarcely be further from the concentrated intensity of *Macbeth*. Some critics, Doctor Johnson among them, have thought the play carelessly constructed. This reaction may have been caused partly by the standard editorial practice of chopping the play into a confusing multiplicity of scenes, some only a few lines long. In the swift continuity of performance on the unlocalised Globe stage a clearer, bolder play emerges. As always, Shakespeare's words create its world. The action (apart from a few brief stopovers) simply swings between Egypt and Rome, each world vividly evoked in the fantasies and fears of the other. It is through the words that the play achieves its famous scope, sweeping over the *ranged empire* – Syria, Lydia, Mesopotamia, Armenia, the Euphrates and the Ionian Sea.

Similarly, it is through the medium of description and suggestion that the obsessive relationship of the lovers is conveyed, so that it can seem both a transcendent love and a degraded tumble on the bed of Ptolemy. Physical sexuality is suggested, by a kind of poetic transference, through the imagery of creatures and inanimate things, the water which follows the beating oars *as amorous of their strokes*, the fishes with Cleopatra's hooks through their *slimy jaws*, the sun which blackens her complexion with its *amorous pinches*, the stroke of death which is like a lover's pinch too – it *hurts and is desired*.

For obvious reasons, Shakespeare's evocative poetry was a specially important gift to the boy-players, the chief method by which they created the illusion of femininity. This is not to underrate their histrionic skills: there must have been a continuous supply of well-trained apprentices, and it is interesting to see how Shakespeare's demands on them developed from the mainly verbal dexterity required of Kate and Juliet, through the emotional sensibility of Beatrice, Rosalind and Viola and the teasing sexuality of Cressida, to Cleopatra. The first player of this part must have been gifted enough for Shakespeare to risk the moment when Cleopatra imagines her love for Antony being guyed on the stage by the quick Roman comedians:

> ... *Antony*
> *Shall be brought drunken forth, and I shall see*
> *Some squeaking Cleopatra boy my greatness*
> *I'th'posture of a whore.*

Although in terms of action Cleopatra's part is relatively short, no female character in Shakespeare is so often and so fully presented to the mind's eye of the audience; she is constantly talked about, and she constantly talks about herself; her *infinite variety* emerges out of a web of comment, excitable gossip, reminiscence. Towards the end, Shakespeare adds an unexpected thread, an elusive play of the ideas of marriage, motherhood, womanliness. And in a small but crucial way he departs from his source: Plutarch, speculating about the manner of her death, repeatedly insists that the bite of the lethal asp was on her arm; Shakespeare deliberately follows another tradition and turns it into a final moment of great tenderness:

> *Peace, peace.*
> *Dost thou not see my baby at my breast*
> *That sucks the nurse asleep?*

The 'book' of *Antony and Cleopatra* was registered with the Stationers' Company in May 1608, at the same time as another, very different play, the tragi-comedy called *Pericles, Prince of Tyre*.[142] No author was named for either, but while there is no doubt that Shakespeare wrote *Antony*, it is as certain as it can reasonably be that he was not the sole author of *Pericles*. This should not be surprising, since the hunger for new plays often resulted in collaboration or revision (it is not always easy to tell the difference). The other contributor was probably George Wilkins, a disreputable figure who was enjoying a brief success as a writer (a George Wilkins, probably the same person, would later testify in the dispute of Belott and Mountjoy). His novel, *The Painful Adventures of Pericles Prince of Tyre* (1608) was explicitly linked to the play performed by the King's Men.[143] Wilkins probably wrote the first part of *Pericles* and offered it to the Company for consideration (they had already put on another play of his); Shakespeare then supplied the rest – more than half the play. But the division is not clear-cut: in among the workaday rhyming verse Wilkins seems to have favoured are some unexpectedly delightful, perhaps Shakespearean, things like the chat of the philosophical fishermen who draw a pretty moral or two as they compare *their watery empire* to the world of men.

The later part of the play is unmistakably Shakespeare's; the sinister, quirky, ruefully comic brothel scenes are his, and no one else could have written the wonderful poetry of loss and renewal in the later Pericles episodes. The sea seems to wash over the play. It is during a tremendous sea-storm that the wife of Pericles dies in *terrible childbed* and his daughter has her chiding nativity. The most celebrated passage is his lament as he prepares to cast the body of his wife into the sea. The strangely tranquil vision of her *lying with simple shells* beneath the humming water recalls Timon's dream of a gravestone washed with the light foam of the sea; and it prefigures the song in *The Tempest* which tells Ferdinand that his father lies five fathom deep.

Pericles was the beginning of a new phase in Shakespeare's work: it is the first of the four late Romances, or Tragicomedies,

plays which, though they are all different, share to some degree a common approach. The plots, with their coincidences and improbabilities, are deliberately artless – *like an old tale still*. The events are driven by a Providence that seems random and is ultimately benevolent. The Gods themselves occasionally intervene. These beautiful plays are much concerned with forgiveness, renewal, the lost which is found again, death and rebirth, the redemption of the old by the clear-eyed young. From time to time the poetry has an other-worldly quality, *a strain of rareness* not quite like anything else in Shakespeare, and at key moments music, sometimes mysterious or supernatural, adds to the *ceremonious, solemn and unearthly* mood.[144] Ben Jonson, who liked the strong meat of classical tragedy and worldly comedy, did not care for these '*Tales, Tempests*, and such like *Drolleries*', and he thought *Pericles* 'a mouldy tale'.[145] But Shakespeare knew what he was doing: *Pericles* was, for a time at least, a popular play.

However, Shakespeare had not yet done with tragedy, or with Plutarch. *Coriolanus*[146] has probably suffered a little in comparison with the splendours of *Antony and Cleopatra*. It is a political play, full of rushing action, which begins at once with the eruption on to the stage of *mutinous citizens* armed with staves and clubs and *resolved rather to die than to famish*. This kind of disturbance was all too familiar to Shakespeare and his audience: in 1607 just such food riots had torn through the Midlands and come close to Stratford. This active first scene is a sort of prologue to the play: the particular issue of hunger is absorbed into the more general conflict which some readers see as the opposition of authority to anarchy, others as the struggle of democracy against brutal power – Brecht regarded the play as a drama of the people betrayed by their fascist leader.[147] As always, Shakespeare has a multiple vision of things.

The play's style has been called flinty, harsh, rugged, gritty; a present-day actor found himself drawn to the part of Coriolanus by his 'tough-leather' way of speaking.[148] The language is certainly sometimes difficult, but it is vigorous, often witty, full of unexpected touches; and it is prevailingly fierce, apt for the play's world in which a patrician's honour is measured by his battle-scars (Coriolanus has 27 wounds, and *every gash was an enemy's grave*). There is plenty of bloodshed during the siege of Corioli, in which the tiring-house doors have a starring role as the city gates; the language of this episode is rich in sanguinary variation: Coriolanus appears *flayed*, he is *mantled*, *smeared*, *masked* in blood, *a thing of blood* who paints the gates of the city and runs *reeking o'er the lives of men*.

There is only one moment of tenderness – when the hero returned from battle finds his wife cannot speak for tears: *My gracious silence, hail ... Ah my dear ...* However this is not the only silence in this noisy play. Towards the end, when Volumnia, the tigress mother of Coriolanus, is sent to dissuade him from attacking Rome, she batters him with one of the longest speeches in Shakespeare, 52 lines of arguing, bullying and pleading. At last, seeing him unmoved (his eye *red as 'twould burn Rome*), she breaks off and with angry irony promises to keep quiet – at least for a time:

> *I am hushed until our city be afire,*
> *And then I'll speak a little.*

And at that moment Shakespeare, who has been following North's Plutarch closely, startlingly strikes out on his own. Plutarch's Coriolanus, seeing his mother kneel, reacts straightaway, crying out to her. But the Coriolanus of the play, before he relents, *holds her by the hand silent*. This famous stage direction marks the turning-point of the tragedy. Evidently Shakespeare, though he worked in an acoustical auditorium and made magic with words, also knew well the theatrical value of silence.

The Great Frost which lasted from December 1607 to February 1608 was unusually cruel, even for the wicked winters of the time. Ships at sea were trapped in ice and there was dancing on the surface of the frozen Thames. On New Year's Eve, Shakespeare's brother Edmund – a player himself and not yet 28 – was buried in the church of St Saviour's in Southwark, 'with a forenoon knell of the great bell'. This was an expensive arrangement and it must have been made by Shakespeare: perhaps he was not, after all, without family feeling. Soon after the melting of the ice, a greater trouble reached London with the return of the plague. The outbreak settled in during the summer of 1608 and it lasted for more than a year; twice during that difficult time Shakespeare's Company received grants of money 'by way of His Majesty's reward for their private practice in the time of infection'.

In spite of this trouble, the Company found themselves able to take an important step. The Blackfriars Children, after one controversial play too many, were in serious disgrace. In any case, their palmy days were over – they could scarcely be thought of as children any more; the 20-year-old William Ostler, for instance, joined the King's Men as an adult player almost at once, and within a couple of years he had married Heminges's daughter Thomasina. A casualty of the Blackfriars disgrace was John

Marston, who found himself in Newgate; he never wrote for the stage again. But for the King's Men it was all benefit. With the Children gone from Blackfriars, the Burbage brothers could at last take possession of the indoor playhouse their father had created; local opposition had faded away for the time being. With two playhouses of their own, the King's Men were indisputably the market leaders. Though the Blackfriars was much smaller than the Globe, admission to it was more expensive, and it drew a more courtly, or more affluent, audience. It turned out a highly profitable investment, and Shakespeare was, of course, one of the seven share-holding housekeepers.

The lease of the new playhouse was signed in August 1608. That autumn Shakespeare was probably back in Stratford for a while. In September a nephew, Michael Hart, was born, and a little later a godson, William Walker, was baptised; he was the son of a sometime Bailiff and would himself hold the office 40 years later. That same September Shakespeare's mother died. She had brought property and status to the Shakespeare family; she had outlived her husband and four of her eight children; and she had seen a great-grandchild born. It is not known whether she clung to the Catholic faith of the greater Arden family; she was buried in the peaceful Protestant churchyard of Holy Trinity.

A well-graced actor leaves the stage
1609–16

It would be pleasant to think that Shakespeare spent some years of tranquil retirement in Stratford. He still owned the Henley Street property, and after their mother's death his sister Joan continued to live there with her husband and three boys, crowded into the western part of the double house; the eastern part had been let some years earlier to one Lewis Hiccox and his quarrelsome wife Alice, and it had become an inn called the Maidenhead. It is reasonable to assume that Anne Shakespeare and Judith, now in her twenties and not yet married, were already living at New Place. Also living there, as guest or tenant, was Thomas Greene, the Town Clerk of Stratford; he may have been a kinsman, since he called Shakespeare 'cousin', and he named his children William and Anne. Greene moved into his own house in the autumn of 1610: it is likely that about then Shakespeare had indicated his intention to settle into New Place himself. There was the Great Garden to occupy him; it was in 1608 that King James, hoping to stimulate a native silk industry, exhorted every Englishman to buy a mulberry tree, and in 1609 that a supply of trees reached Warwickshire.

Small-town life among his family and friends – Sadlers, Quineys, Combes, Greenes – would be very different from the high-pressure existence of the playhouse, let alone the excitements of Rebellion and Plot. Stratford affairs were ambling along: in

1611, Shakespeare's name was added (as if he was a recent arrival) to the list of townsmen willing to contribute to the cost of 'prosecuting the Bill in Parliament for the better repair of the highways'. However, unlike his father, he did not concern himself with the business of town government. The increasingly Puritan Corporation might in any case have jibbed at the idea of an Alderman with theatrical connections. But he cannot have been thought wholly ungodly: he entertained a visiting preacher at New Place, and in return the Council reimbursed him for a quart of sack and a quart of claret wine. The *quiet life*, according to the princely boys in *Cymbeline*, may be a prison and a cage to aspiring youth, but it is appropriate to *stiff age*.

In fact, however, this pleasant picture is not the whole truth. Shakespeare was still a man of the theatre and could be said not to have retired at all in the modern sense. He may well have given up the day-to-day business of acting by 1609 – records of his work as a professional actor are in any case sparse. That he did some acting is certain: he was certainly a player in 1592 when Greene attacked him; in the printed editions of Jonson's plays he is included among the Principal Comedians in *Every Man in his Humour* (1598) and the Principal Tragedians in *Sejanus* (1603); in the First Folio his name heads the list of Principal Actors in his own plays. We do not know what kind of actor he was. Chettle praised his excellence. An epigram of 1610 tells us that he played 'kingly parts'.[149] According to stories that surfaced later he was Adam in *As You Like It* and the Ghost in *Hamlet* – other parts assigned to him by biographers are imaginative guesses or suggestions.[150] He was said to be a better poet than actor, but Aubrey heard that he 'did act exceedingly well', and he added that 'B.Jonson was never a good actor, but an excellent instructor'.

Whether in Stratford or London, Shakespeare continued to work, and though he slowed down a little, there was no lessening of creative energy. Between 1609 and 1611 he wrote the three Romances, *Cymbeline*, *The Winter's Tale* and *The Tempest*,[151] each in its own way a new and startling venture. The story of *Cymbeline* is so intricately woven that, to unravel the plot, the last scene has to deliver no less than 24 revelations (*more matter still*, remarks Cymbeline after the eighth surprise). The plotting of *The Winter's Tale*, on the other hand, is simple, but it is no less astonishing: the contrasting halves of the play are divided by a gap of 16 years, boldly spanned in a single choric speech delivered by Time himself. The play's great surprise has the whole final scene to itself, and the revelation – that the statue of Queen Hermione, supposed dead 16 years earlier, is actually the still living Queen herself – is so beautiful as to make the suggestion of improbability irrelevant.

The language of the late Romances, too, is often adventurous, and sometimes, especially in *Cymbeline*, odd and difficult. In all three plays Shakespeare drives coherence to its limits in order to convey strong feeling, for instance Innogen's longing to see her husband Posthumus again:

Then, true Pisanio,
Who long'st like me to see thy lord, who long'st –
O let me bate – but not like me – yet long'st
But in a fainter – O, not like me,
For mine's beyond beyond …

He seems to be trying out new tones. Wholly different from Innogen's rapturous flow is the magically slow movement of the verse as Hermione's statue stirs into life (the expressive colons are in the Folio text):

Music; awake her: strike:

A mezzotint after the Chandos portrait of William Shakespeare

'Tis time: descend: be stone no more: approach:
Strike all that look upon with marvel: come:
I'll fill your grave up: stir: nay, come away:
Bequeath to Death your numbness: for from him,
Dear Life redeems you …

It is not entirely surprising that some readers have seen these redemption stories as Christian, indeed Catholic, works. A statute of 1606 made it an offence to 'speak or use the holy name of God' in any kind of play or performance; but Jupiter or 'the Heavens' or Providence could stand in for the Deity. All three plays reach resolution in penitence, forgiveness, reconciliation. But Shakespeare had not exorcised the ghost of tragedy: final harmony is not reached without suffering, and *Providence divine* is cruel for a purpose. Jupiter tells the reproachful ghosts who question his justice, *Whom best I love I cross*. Hermione, resigning herself to unjust imprisonment, knows her suffering is *for my better grace*. The word 'grace' has theological resonance; the gods pour grace from *sacred vials*; in an almost explicit reference to the same idea Prospero speaks, with an echo of the Mass, of the *sweet aspersion* which *the heavens let fall*.

Of course the Romances are not unremittingly solemn, any more than they are wholly fantastical. The real world that Shakespeare knew is always present, and not just to provide comic contrast. In *The Winter's Tale* the pretty pastoral love of Perdita and Florizel is set in a recognizable countryside, a domestic world of warden pies and tods of wool and girls whispering by the kiln-hole. The Old Shepherd could well be describing a jolly lady of Snitterfield or Shottery as he remembers how his wife enjoyed being mistress of the feast –

her face afire
With labour, and the thing she took to quench it.

The old man himself perhaps had a prototype in Richard Hathaway's shepherd, Thomas Whittington, who outlived his master by 20 years and in his will left 'unto the poor people of Stratford 40 shillings that is in the hand of Anne Shakespeare'. The essential spirit of misrule in this countryside is provided by Autolycus, clown, pedlar and crook; he both delights the country people and preys on them – and in passing steals the sheets bleaching on the hedge. Such rogues, according to William Harrison, made mischief everywhere and were 'often stocked and whipped' or even 'eaten up by the gallows'. It was a brilliant part for Robert Armin.

Caliban in *The Tempest* is a more complicated kind of maverick. In a sense he is a product of his time: English colonisation of the New World had begun, and there were stories of strange savages encountered in the wilderness; indeed, from time to time 'savages' of a not very formidable kind were brought to London: Manteo, who taught the learned Thomas Hariot his language; Princess Pocahontas, who went to court and saw one of Ben Jonson's entertainments. In our day, Caliban has been seen as the archetypal victim of racialist colonialism.[152] It is impossible to tell whether Shakespeare sympathised with the pioneers who genuinely believed they were bringing the gifts of civilisation and true religion to primitive people, or with those who openly asserted that 'our first work is the expulsion of the savages to gain the free range of the country ... for it is infinitely better to have no heathen among us, who at best were but thorns in our sides'.[153]

On its way to the New World in 1610, the *Sea Venture* was stranded on rocks off Bermuda. The island had always been avoided as dangerous and devil-haunted, but the ship's company found it hospitable and commodious, even though it was without the benefit of human cultivation. Accounts of this adventure, which seemed to give the nature-nurture debate a real and topical context, provided Shakespeare with material for *The Tempest*.

Perhaps it is more sensible to see Caliban in the context of ideas about the relationship of Nature and Civilisation, the old debate about whether nurture, civility, art and grace lift nature above its primitive self, or whether *great creating nature* is corrupted and 'bastardized'[154] by the intervention of man. This debate, a staple of pastoral poetry, surfaces in all these Romances: Perdita dismisses *carnations and streaked gillyvors* (flowers modified by cross-breeding) *ature's bastards*. Caliban is *a born devil*, and in his state of nature, defying nurture, he remains a *thing of darkness*, a brutal monster with *a very ancient and fish-like smell*; but he also has his own kind of dignity, a fierce sense of dispossession and even moments of pathos. Cloten in *Cymbeline*, on the other hand, is nurtured in the court, but he too is born wicked, and he remains lustful and brutish – and he refuses to change his shirt though he reeks like a sacrifice. Cloten comes to a sticky end; Caliban at the close of his story resolves to *seek for grace*. Yet again, Shakespeare's vision is not simple.

The Tempest was the last play to be written wholly by Shakespeare. It was presented before the King on Hallowmas Night, 1 November 1611, and a few months later Shakespeare turned 48, the age he gives the *ancient ruffian* Kent in *King Lear*. His daughters were grown up and his granddaughter already four years old; a hopeful affection for a younger generation seems to be reflected in the Romances, and especially in the spirited heroines to whom Shakespeare gave such expressive names. *The Tempest* has sometimes been seen as an aging dramatist's farewell to the theatre, with a hint of Shakespeare himself in the Prospero who grandly renounces his art and, not without a touch of regret, leaves his enchanted island:

In the Folio the name Innogen, with its connotation of innocence, is spelt *Imogen*, but this is usually thought to be a simple misreading of the copy text: the name is *Innogen* in Holinshed, Shakespeare's source, as well as in an eyewitness account of a 1611 performance, and in Shakespeare's only other use of it (a stage direction in *Much Ado*). The familiar modern name derives from the popularity of *Cymbeline* (just as Wendy was born out of *Peter Pan*). It is curious to think that it is probably the result of a printer's error.

Every third thought shall be my grave. The play's most famous lines dwell on the transience of life, and the imagery is of dreams and the *insubstantial pageant* of the theatre.

But Shakespeare was no Prospero; far from renouncing his art he had a hand in writing three more plays. For *The Two Noble Kinsmen* and a play, now lost, called *Cardenio*, his collaborator was John Fletcher (1579–1625), and it is highly likely that Fletcher was also part-author of *All Is True*, to which the Folio editors gave the now usually accepted name *Henry VIII*.[155] For some years Fletcher had been working with Francis Beaumont (1584–1616) in a famously successful partnership: according to Aubrey 'there was a wonderful consimility of fancy' between the two writers, and 'they lived together on the Bankside, not far from the playhouse, both bachelors; lay together; had one wench in the house between them …' Their elaborate tragicomedy *Philaster, or Love Lies A-Bleeding*, written for the King's Men, helped to create the fashion which produced Shakespeare's own Romances. Beaumont gave up writing in 1613; Fletcher went on to become Shakespeare's successor as chief dramatist for the King's Men.

During the winter of 1612–13 the Company was extraordinarily busy at the court, which seemed to be caught up in a tragicomedy of its own. In November the young and hopeful Prince Henry died of typhoid fever – the King, grieving and horrified, could not bear to stay by his dying son. But the same year also saw the betrothal of the Princess Elizabeth to Frederick, Elector Palatine, an event which called for a season of specially energetic revelling. That winter the Company played twenty times at court, presenting some of Shakespeare's earlier plays as well as *The Winter's Tale*, *The Tempest* (with its nuptial masque), *Cardenio* and two performances of *Philaster*. The wedding itself took place on St Valentine's Day, 14 February 1613 – John Donne wrote a gorgeous *Epithalamion* celebrating the happy couple as 'two Phoenixes'. The week-long junketing was as disorderly as it was lavish: a masque specially written by Beaumont had to be postponed because the Banqueting House at Whitehall was so crowded that the performers could not push their way in; moreover the King was too 'wearied and sleepy' to remain.

Henry VIII might be thought a play well fitted for this time of rejoicing: it is full of royal splendours, pageantry, ceremonial processions. Henry is not the bloat king of Charles Laughton, but young and volatile. The story covers the period of his divorce from Katherine of Aragon, the wooing and wedding of Anne Bullen (or Boleyn), and the birth of the infant who is to become Elizabeth I; and it ends with a prophetic compliment not only to her but also to her successor James:

> *Wherever the bright sun of heaven shall shine,*
> *His honour and the greatness of his name*
> *Shall be, and make new nations. He shall flourish,*
> *And like a mountain cedar reach his branches*
> *To all the plains about him.*

Nevertheless, for all the splendour, the general effect is sombre: while the King pursues his self-willed purpose, three great figures, Buckingham, Wolsey and Katherine, are swept away; and each fall is in its own way tragic. It is widely agreed (there is some dissent) that the most memorable passages are Fletcher's; they include the final prophecy and also Wolsey's famous *Farewell, a long farewell, to all my greatness*.[156]

In comparison with Fletcher's easy and melodious verse, some of Shakespeare's language seems tangled and obscure, as if he scarcely cared whether the listeners understood it or not.[157] But the solemnity of the play is lit up by some authentically Shakespearean sparks too, as when Wolsey vents his irritation at the King's plan:

> *Anne Bullen? No, I'll no Anne Bullens for him.*
> *There's more in't than fair visage. Bullen?*

No, we'll no Bullens ...

And of course there is still plenty of powerful writing, for instance in the scene, a great one even by Shakespeare's own standards, where Queen Katherine pleads her case to the King, and unleashes her magnificent rage on Wolsey.

The Two Noble Kinsmen is a return to romance. The story comes from Chaucer's *Knight's Tale*, and its subject is an old favourite, the conflict of friendship and love. As in *Henry VIII*, some of the most pleasing passages are Fletcher's, including the vignette of a Schoolmaster with something of Holofernes in him: preparing his rustics to present a masque for the Duke, he patiently instructs an actor dressed as a baboon:

My friend, carry your tail without offence
Or scandal to the ladies ...
And when you bark, do it with judgment ...

Once again, beside the amiability of Fletcher, Shakespeare's language can seem impenetrable:

Yet what man
Thirds his own worth – the case is each of ours –
When that his action's dregged with mind assured
'Tis bad he goes about.

Sometimes this strangeness is put to dramatic use. Chaucer's description of the Temple of Mars, one of his masterpieces, is frightening in the specificity of its images – a suicide, his hair matted with blood, a sow devouring a child in its cradle, a corpse lying in a bush with throat carved open. Shakespeare, in Arcite's prayer to Mars, goes for a different kind of power, grand, strange, nightmarish: the god of war turns green Neptune to purple, plucks masoned turrets from the blue clouds, cures the world of the plurisy of people. Another of the haunting passages is Shakespeare's picture of old age (curiously included in a prayer to Venus):

The aged cramp
Had screwed his square foot round,
The gout had knit his fingers into knots,
Torturing convulsions from his globy eyes
Had almost drawn their spheres …

Chaucer's poem ends with Duke Theseus serenely reflecting on the wisdom that makes virtue of necessity and recognises that we should take that well which we cannot eschew. The play, too, ends stoically, on a note of calm acceptance. The closing lines are addressed by Theseus to the uncaring gods, and they are perhaps the last that Shakespeare wrote for the stage:

What things you make of us! For what we lack
We laugh, for what we have are sorry; still
Are children in some kind. Let us be thankful
For that which is, and with you leave dispute
That are above our question. Let's go off
And bear us like the time.

In the Prologue to *The Two Noble Kinsmen* there is a reference to *our losses*, not a merely conventional phrase, but an allusion to a real and formidable loss. On 29 June 1613, the feast day of St Peter and St Paul, the Globe, 'the glory of the Bank',[158] was destroyed by fire. The King's Men were presenting *Henry VIII*, still a new play, and the spectators, 'attentive to the show', did not notice that the wadding ('tamplin or stopple') of a ceremonial cannon had lodged, still smouldering, in the playhouse thatch. The building was consumed in less than two hours. It was said that by the fair grace of God there were no casualties, except for a man whose breeches caught fire – he would have been 'broiled' but that he put the flames out with ale. An anonymous ballad described, with some improbable rhymes, how knights and lords lost hats and swords, and how Burbage came running from the theatre:

'Then with swollen eyes like drunken Flemings
Distressed stood old stuttering Heminges.'[159]

Perhaps it was the businesslike Heminges who made sure playbooks were saved. It would not have been surprising if, after this disaster, the Company had simply transferred to the Blackfriars; but they at once demonstrated their faith in the open amphitheatrical playhouse they knew by rebuilding it. The second Globe was in use a year later.

But although the Globe still had years of success ahead of it, the seeds of change had already been sown. The genius of the new age was the architect and designer Inigo Jones (1573–1652), and it was on the court masque that he lavished his theatrical gift. Masques had always offered the delights of dancing and music; now they became more and more elaborate. The cardinal virtues were extravagance, ingenuity and surprise. Costumes were designed to amaze – in the contrasting antimasques dancers appeared as satyrs, monkeys, hags with rats on their heads, bottles, and, scattering sweet water, as rain. Jones sometimes used a kind of proscenium arch to frame his stage picture, and his scenic spectacles included perspectives in the Italian manner (he visited the Teatro Olimpico in Vicenza and saw its ravishing perspectives). He designed innovative machinery: masquers leapt out of a turning microcosm or globe, or descended from clouds, gracefully and 'not after the stale downright perpendicular fashion, like a bucket into a well'.[160] Scenery wing-pieces moved on grooves above and below. A cliff opened to reveal a palace which in turn opened to discover Oberon in a chariot drawn by white bears. Francis Bacon declared that these 'alterations of scenes, so it be quietly and without noise, are things of great beauty and pleasure', and he liked them to 'abound with light, specially coloured and varied'.[161] Theatrical lighting had arrived; candle-flames shone through glasses of coloured water: ammonia salt turned filtered water sapphire blue; the addition of saffron turned the sapphire to emerald.

There is no reason to think Shakespeare disapproved. His late plays are full of spectacle – a dance of satyrs, a Masque of Goddesses, an antimasque of dogs and hounds, Jupiter descending in thunder and lightning. There are enjoyable mechanical devices: in *The Two Noble Kinsmen* a silver hind on the altar of Venus conveys sweet odours and disappears as a rose-tree ascends in its place; in *The Tempest*, an enticing magic banquet suddenly vanishes *with a quaint device* when Ariel descends like a harpy and claps his wings. Ben Jonson, however, although he had worked closely with Inigo Jones, did come ultimately to disapprove – he seemed to see that an era was ending. With passionate irony he lamented that in the masque poetry had already been ousted by spectacle:

'Painting and carpentry are the soul of Masque.
Pack with your peddling poetry to the stage,
This is the money-get, mechanic age.'[162]

It seemed that the essentially poetic convention, which Shakespeare had helped to develop, and of which he was the master, was already beginning its decline. Soon the tradition would be given a death-blow. At the beginning of the Civil War, the Puritans closed the playhouses, and on 15 April 1644, Matthew Brend demolished the Globe, which stood on the land once owned by his father. When theatres appeared again at the Restoration it was clear that the method of the open Shakespearean playhouse had given way to the different enchantment of the scenery theatre. As a writer in that brave new world declared, the playhouses of Shakespeare's time 'were but plain and simple, with no scenes, nor decorations of the stage, but only old tapestry …'.[163]

The building of the second Globe was expensive – it cost more than £1,000. It was at this time, perhaps, that Shakespeare disposed of his Company shares (he was certainly no longer in possession of them when he made his will). A few months before the fire he had laid out a large sum to buy, at last, a London property, a 'dwelling house' in Blackfriars, built partly over 'a great gate'. It was a house with a past, with 'sundry back doors' and 'dark corners' and 'secret passages towards the water'; priests had hidden there. Previous owners included a kinswoman of Edmund Campion and a crypto-Catholic Bishop of Ely. Shakespeare's purchase was not straight-forward. Associated with him were three trustees (Heminges was one of them) who were nominally co-purchasers, but Shakespeare alone provided the money, part of it by way of a mortgage. We do not know why he thought this device necessary, but it may be relevant that a widow had no automatic right of inheritance if her husband was not sole owner of his property. Shakespeare may have regarded the gatehouse simply as another investment; at the time of his death 'one John Robinson' was living there, presum-ably as a tenant. But he may have intended it as his own foothold in London, all the more useful if he had decided to spend most of his time in Stratford.

His retirement had its irritations. In the summer of 1614 an unpleasant storm broke out over plans to enclose land near Welcombe, to the north of Stratford. Enclosure of open land to create pasture for sheep or cattle caused much bitterness: it could lead to eviction of tenants and unemployment. But these evils may not have been quite as prevalent as the rage of the pamphleteers suggests; enclosing landlords were sometimes convenient scape-goats for more general economic problems.[164] Town opposition to the Welcombe enclosure plan was led by Thomas Greene; the most persistent enclosing landowner was William Combe, nephew to Shakespeare's old friend, the money-lender John Combe.

Shakespeare tried to keep clear of the dispute: he made a separate agreement with the landowners to ensure that at any rate his interest in the tithes collected in the area would not suffer. Although Greene, a tithe-holder too, was included in this agreement, he was not convinced, and in November he met 'my cousin Shakespeare' in London and asked for reassurance. Shake-speare told him there was no immediate cause to worry and that nothing would happen before April; indeed, wrote Greene, 'he and Mr Hall say they think nothing will be done at all'. They were wrong. Combe began digging trenches for his enclosure soon after Christmas; women and children from the town turned out to fill them in. The warfare dragged on, to end in Combe's defeat three years after Shakespeare's death.

Trouble seemed to pursue Shakespeare's daughters. In July 1613 Susanna was in court, suing a certain John Lane for slander: he had put it about that she was an adulteress and that she had 'the running of the reins' – probably a venereal infection (the reins were the kidneys). The slander petered out; Lane failed to appear in court and was excommunicated. Judith was more unfortunate. In February 1616 she married Thomas Quiney, son of the Richard who had once hoped Shakespeare would lend him £30, grandson of the Adrian who was fined for his dung-heap in Henley Street. Judith and her husband were briefly in trouble for marrying in Lent; they probably did so because Thomas thought it wise not to wait: in March he was summoned to the Church Court and there confessed to having got one Margaret Wheeler with child; she gave birth a few days before the trial, and both she and her baby died. Thomas was sentenced to do humiliating public penance, but in the end he escaped with a fine of five shillings and a private expression of penitence.

At the time of this sad affair Shakespeare was approaching 52 years of age. He was the longest-lived of Mary Shakespeare's sons (Gilbert had died in 1612, Richard in 1613), and probably his health was beginning to fail. In January the lawyer Francis Collins drew up the first draft of his will, and on 25 March, the first day of the new year, produced a second version; Shakespeare signed each of its three sheets. This redrafting may have reflected his disappointment in his new son-in-law – Quiney came to trial the day after the will was signed. He is never mentioned in the document (at one point, indeed, Collins began to write 'my son-in-law' and struck it out). Judith, however, is treated quite generously, though part of the sum left to her is made subject to conditions, one of them evidently designed to protect her inheritance from an improvident husband. As a more personal token she also received her father's 'broad silver gilt bowl'. The rest of his plate went to his grand-daughter Elizabeth. To his sister Joan he left £20, all his 'wearing apparel' and the right to remain in the Henley Street house at the nominal rent of a shilling a year; she lived there until her death in 1646 – her husband died just a week before Shakespeare himself. Her sons were remembered in Shakespeare's will too, with £5 apiece (however, he, or the lawyer, forgot the name of one of the boys and had to leave a blank space).

There was a gift of 20 shillings in gold for his little godson William Walker; his sword went to Thomas Combe, brother and supporter of the enclosing landowner. Among the friends he chose to remember with small bequests were Burbage, Heminges and Condell; his old friend Hamnet Sadler; Anthony Nash, whose son would one day marry Shakespeare's granddaughter. And to the poor of Stratford he bequeathed £10.

The most famous item in the will, apparently an insertion into the final draft, is the bequest to his wife of 'my second best bed with all the furniture' (that is, the cover, hangings and so on). Opinion is divided about whether or not this was intended as a deliberate slight to Anne. The early biographers, perhaps unable to believe their eyes, misread the bequest to refer to 'my *brown* best bed' – Malone dryly commented that 'modern editors have been more bountiful to Mrs Shakespeare' than her husband was. It has been suggested that as his wife she would automatically receive a proportion of his goods; that Shakespeare knew she would be looked after by the Hall family;[165] that she herself asked for the bed, since it came from her Shottery home.[166] There is no other mention of her in the will, no word of affection. But then the whole document is businesslike, and entirely without the kind of personal testimony sometimes found in wills of the time.[167] Even at this moment Shakespeare left no clue to his feelings.

However, there does emerge a kind of dynastic determination that his estate should be kept intact and should pass down through the Shakespeares that followed. Apart from the minor bequests, everything – New Place, the Blackfriars house, all his land and fortune – went to Susanna; and the legacy was so directed that it should continue to pass down through male heirs, Susanna's in the first instance, and in default of her issue, Elizabeth's, and finally Judith's. But genetic reality defeated Shakespeare's purpose; Susanna had no sons; Elizabeth had no children; Judith's three boys (the eldest was named Shakespeare Quiney) all died young.

Shakespeare lived on for some weeks after signing his will, and it is not known what cause brought about his death.[168] Typhoid fever is certainly a possibility. There is a story, which did not surface till the 1660s, that 'Shakespeare, Drayton and Ben Jonson had a merry meeting, and it seems drank too hard, for Shakespeare died of a fever there contracted'.[169] He died on 23 April 1616, and he was buried two days later in the chancel of Holy Trinity Church. His gravestone bears a minatory little verse, said to have been written by himself:

Good friend for Jesus sake forbear,
To dig the dust enclosed here:
Blest be the man that spares these stones,
And curst be he that moves my bones.

The memorials and the things of fame 1623

Anne Shakespeare outlived her husband by seven years; on 8 August 1623, she was buried beside him in the chancel of Stratford Church. On her gravestone is a Latin epitaph, which must have been placed there by Susanna: 'Mother, you gave me the breast, milk, life: for these gifts I repay you with a stone ... Come quickly, Christ, that my mother, imprisoned in this grave, may rise again and seek the stars.' Susanna lies to the other side of her father – she died in 1649. Her epitaph is in English verse:

'Witty above her sex, but that's not all,
Wise to salvation was good Mistress Hall,
Something of Shakespeare was in that ...'

Nearby, challengingly, or perhaps blankly, gazing across the chancel from its north wall, is the familiar monument to Shakespeare himself, said to be the work of Gheerart Janssen (or Garrat Johnson). It asserts Shakespeare's formal status of Gentleman: it is crowned with his coat of arms, surmounted by a skull and flanked by naked cherubs representing Labour and Rest. But the quill and paper present him as writer, and the two inscriptions below the half-length figure celebrate his genius: the first, in Latin, compares him with Nestor for discernment, Socrates for genius, Virgil for art; the English verse entreats the hurrying Passenger to stay a moment and remember the poet whose art lives on though with

William Shakespeare's memorial in Stratford Church

him 'quick Nature died'. Janssen's monument was probably in place before Anne's death.

Later in that same year, 1623, there appeared the most significant tribute to Shakespeare's genius, the First Folio edition of his collected plays. As epoch-making books go, it is not particularly rare;[170] something like 1,000 copies were printed and more than 200 of them still survive. And it was not without precedent: seven years earlier Ben Jonson had published his *Works* in Folio, staking the claim for his stage writing, no less than his poems, to be taken seriously as literature. It was a long way from the early days of Shakespeare's career, when plays were largely treated as raw material for an expanding industry.[171] The editors of the Shakespeare Folio, Heminges and Condell, were evidently in no doubt about the importance of the plays, even though, with conventional deprecation, they called them 'trifles' in their letter dedicating the book to the Earls of Pembroke and Montgomery. These 'most noble and incomparable brethren' were happily chosen as dedicatees: they were the sons of the Countess of Pembroke, Sir Philip Sidney's sister and Nashe's 'second Minerva'; in 1623 the theatre-loving Pembroke (who may have been the model for the Fair Youth of the Sonnets) was Lord Chamberlain; his brother succeeded him in that post, and the Beaumont and Fletcher Folio (1647) was dedicated to him.

Heminges and Condell undertook their work 'without ambition either of self-profit or fame'; they wished 'only to keep the memory of so worthy a friend and fellow alive, as was our Shakespeare'. Their declared aim was to publish his plays 'according to the true original copies', and to clear away the errors caused by the publication of 'stolen and surreptitious' texts. Inevitably they did not wholly succeed, since the printers worked from difficult copy material – published texts, playbooks, manuscripts in various stages of transmission. But they managed to bring together all the plays now attributed to Shakespeare, except *Pericles*, *The Two*

Noble Kinsmen and (of course) *Cardenio*. Moreover, of the 36 Folio plays, 18 had not been published before and would probably have been lost, like so many plays of the period, but for the enterprise of Heminges and Condell. To them we owe the preservation of, for example, the three late Romances, *Julius Caesar, As You Like It, Twelfth Night, Macbeth* and *Antony and Cleopatra*. Theirs was an ambitious, difficult and very expensive project, and happily it must have been a success: within ten years a Second Folio was published, and two more appeared before the end of the century. The inclusion within a single volume of almost all Shakespeare's work for the stage made it possible for a reader to see the scope of his genius, and with the appearance of the First Folio, it could be said, the cult of Shakespeare began.

Included among the prefatory material in the volume is Ben Jonson's tribute, *To the memory of my beloved, the AUTHOR Mr William Shakespeare and what he hath left us*. This wonderful poem is charged with personal affection, and it is also a grand celebration of Shakespeare's genius as a dramatist, outshining the remembered wits of his young days, Lyly, 'sporting Kyd' and Marlowe of the 'mighty line'; he ranks with the immortals of the ancient world, like 'thund'ring Aeschylus' – indeed, compared with him, 'the merry Greek, tart Aristophanes, neat Terence, witty Plautus' seem to lie antiquated and deserted.

Jonson was not always so whole-hearted in his admiration for Shakespeare: he loved him and honoured his memory 'on this side idolatry'. He certainly helped to perpetuate certain myths: that Shakespeare was under-educated, with 'small Latin, and less Greek'; that he wrote quickly and undiscriminatingly, by instinct rather than by art – when Jonson heard Shakespeare praised for never blotting a line, he acidly responded, 'Would he had blotted a thousand.' The idea of the under-educated Shakespeare was exploded long ago. However, the suggestion that he wrote with unusual facility may have more substance: according to Heminges and Condell, 'his mind and hand went together', and he uttered what he thought with such 'easiness' that there was scarcely 'a blot in his papers'. But he was certainly also a conscious artist, slower in turning out plays than some of his contemporaries, and there is some evidence that he revised his work. In his Folio tribute Jonson partly gainsays his own accusation, declaring that the poet who aims 'to write a living line must sweat' in the turning of his verses:

'For a good Poet's made, as well as born.
And such wert thou.'

On the title-page of the Folio is the portrait of Shakespeare engraved by Martin Droeshout (there were two artists of that name, uncle and nephew; this is probably the younger). It is an awkward portrait, and oddly unreal – the artist has had difficulty with proportion. Nevertheless, the Droeshout engraving and the Janssen memorial are the only certainly authentic images of Shakespeare we have. Though both were made after his death, both must have been seen by his family and friends, and at least nobody is on record as having complained. Of the two, the monument is probably nearer the truth; at least it seems to depict a real person, and the fact that it is not conventionally 'poetic' may even suggest a greater actuality. However, the absence from both images of any hint of the poet's fine frenzy has disappointed some admirers of Shakespeare; there may even be a faint touch of snobbery in the way occupations thought to be anti-poetic are foisted on the depicted sitter: the face in the engraving has been said to resemble a balding commercial traveller; the monument has been thought to look like an accountant rather than an artist; it has the face of an affluent and self-satisfied pork-butcher. By comparison, the Grafton portrait (which may not be of Shakespeare at all) seems to symbolise the Essential Poet.[172] The Chandos portrait, the

The Droeshout portrait of Shakespeare from the title page of the First Folio

founding picture of the National Portrait Gallery, is more attractive, but its claim to authenticity (it may once have belonged to Davenant) is not quite beyond doubt.[173]

The fact is that we do not know precisely what Shakespeare was like, either in appearance or in temperament. Aubrey heard that 'he was a handsome, well-shaped man: very good company, and of a very ready and pleasant smooth wit'. He seems never to have quarrelled, even with the quarrelsome Jonson. Among contemporary references to him there are epithets of an amiable and general kind, like 'friendly' and 'gentle'; Chettle called him civil, upright, honest; Jonson thought him honest, open, free. But this same free and open fellow was ready to hoard malt in hard times and to evade requests for help when enclosure threatened his town. It seems that he could be affectionate: Robert Davenant, William's brother, cherished the childhood memory of 'a hundred kisses' from him. But silence about his family – his wife, his son who died young – is a puzzle. Perhaps he was simply what is now called (usually in a tone of admiration) a very private man.

His concealment of his emotional self was certainly successful, and may have been deliberate, perhaps related to his incomparable gift of imagining other selves. That his empathetic understanding was a special gift was soon recognised: in one of the earliest assessments of Shakespeare the dramatist, the literary Duchess of Newcastle made it a theme: 'one would think he had been transformed into every one of those persons he hath described' – clown, king, coward, well-bred man, drunkard, madman, knave – 'nay, one would think that he had been metamorphosed from a man to a woman, for who could describe Cleopatra better … ?'[174] It is not in the least surprising that his plays and poems have been ransacked for what they can tell about the man: recent biographers have seen in his writing reflections of his dissatisfaction with himself, or of some inner pain; of his innate qualities of constancy, loyalty and self-respect; of his sexual jealousy, sexual guilt, sexual diffidence; of his belief in human love as a spiritual ideal. Inferences of this kind may indeed be valid, but they can also be ambiguous, even contradictory: on the evidence of his writing Shakespeare has been seen both as a believer in order and authority, and as a subversive; as a typical product of a male-dominated society, and as a proto-feminist; as a Catholic and as a sceptic; as a generous moralist, and as one who 'seems to write without any moral purpose'.[175]

The cult of Shakespeare has put the glover's son through some curious transformations. The composer Richard Wagner, during his boyhood, was inspired by seeing the face of Beethoven in the portrait lithographs that were everywhere: 'I soon conceived an image of him as a sublime and unique supernatural being ... this image was associated in my brain with that of Shakespeare; in ecstatic dreams I met both of them, saw and spoke to them, and on awakening found myself bathed in tears'.[176] It is hard to imagine what Mary Shakespeare, or Jonson, or Doctor Hall, would have made of this ecstasy. Of course the picture of Shakespeare changes as times change, and of course there is loss. The fate of the Janssen monument makes an apt analogy. For a time it was presumably accepted as a tolerable likeness, but by 1748 it had become 'much impaired and decayed', and a painter was engaged to 'repair and beautify' it. Half a century later, Malone, father of Shakespeare biography, had the whole thing painted 'a good stone-colour', presumably because he thought the restored colours inappropriate or improbable – at any rate he believed he was returning the sculpture to its original state. Seventy years later, Malone's over-painting was removed in its turn and the monument was once more given new colours.[177] Now after all these transformations, and yet another wide gap of time, we can only guess at what Shakespeare's image originally looked like.

Notes

Chapter Titles: *Love's Labour's Lost* V.ii.585; *Twelfth Night* I.v.154; *Julius Caesar* II.i.22; *Venus and Adonis* 967; *Hamlet* III.ii.265; *Hamlet* II.ii.331; *Henry V* II Chorus 36; *The Merchant of Venice* II.ii.103; *All's Well That Ends Well* II.iii.35; *Richard II* V.ii.24; *Twelfth Night* III.iii.23.

1 E K Chambers, in *William Shakespeare, A Study of Facts and Problems* (Oxford: 1930) vol 1, p 9 (hereafter Chambers, *Shakespeare*), notes that a survey of 1582 recorded 'a vast number' of elms.

2 The business of a whittawer was to 'taw', or dress, hides to make 'whitleather', soft white leather (OED).

3 Park Honan, *Shakespeare: A Life* (Oxford: 1999) pp 37f, hereafter Honan, *Shakespeare*.

4 Quoted by Mark Eccles, *Shakespeare in Warwickshire* (Madison, Wisconsin: 1963) p 39, hereafter Eccles, *Warwickshire*.

5 Richard Jones, *The Birth of Mankind* (1540). This is a translation of a treatise by Eucharius Röesslin, City Physician of Worms. Quoted in *The Thought and Culture of the English Renaissance*, ed Elizabeth M Nugent (Cambridge: 1956) pp 292f.

6 Thomas Middleton, *The Mayor of Quinborough*.

7 E K Chambers, *The Elizabethan Stage* (Oxford: 1923) vol 2, p 83, hereafter Chambers, *Stage*.

8 Christopher Tyerman, *A History of Harrow School* (Oxford: 2000) p 25.

9 Honan, *Shakespeare*, pp 14f.

10 Eccles, *Warwickshire*, p 52.

11 J Huizinga, *Erasmus of Rotterdam* (New York: 1924) p 115.

12 Michael Drayton, *To my most dearly-loved friend Henry Reynolds, Esquire, of Poets and Poesy* (1627).

13 John Brinsley, *Ludus Literarius, or The Grammar School*, 1612. Quoted in *Shakespeare's England*, ed R E Pritchard (Stroud: 1999) pp 94f.

14 M St Clare Byrne, *Elizabethan Life in Town and Country* (London: 1925) p 202.

15 Sir Ernest Barker, *Traditions of Civility* (Cambridge: 1948) pp 155f.

16 *Aubrey's Brief Lives*, ed Oliver Lawson Dick (Harmondsworth: 1962) pp 3, 49, first published London, 1949; Maurice Balme, *Two Antiquaries* (Durham: 2001).

17 E K Chambers, *Shakespearean Gleanings* (Oxford: 1944) p 52. It was common for names to appear in variant forms.

18 Alice Hogge, *God's Secret Agents* (London: 2005) p 173; Michael Wood, *In Search of Shakespeare* (London: 2003) pp 158–61, 171–4.

19 S Schoenbaum, in *William Shakespeare: A Compact Documentary Life* (Oxford: 1977) p 47, quotes extensively from the Testament.

20 Quoted in George C Odell, *Shakespeare – from Betterton to Irving* (New York: 1920) vol 1, p 348.

21 The painter Maurice Percival in a letter to Ronald Watkins, 16 May 1961.

22 Conrad Russell, *The Crisis of Parliaments* (Oxford: 1971) p 12, notes that in the Devonshire village of Colyton a

third of first children were probably conceived before marriage.

23 James Joyce, *Ulysses* (London: 1960) p 260. First published Paris, 1922.

24 This reading of Sonnet 145 was explored by Andrew Gurr (*Essays in Criticism,* 1971), and is accessibly explained in his *William Shakespeare* (London: 1995) p 24.

25 G W Prothero, *Select Statutes and other Constitutional Documents* (Oxford: 1954) p 67. First published 1894

26 Chambers, *Stage*, vol 2, pp 87f.

27 S Schoenbaum, *Shakespeare's Lives* (Oxford: 1970) pp 108–14, hereafter Schoenbaum, *Lives*.

28 Thomas Nashe, *Strange News* (1593).

29 John Stow, *A Survey of London* (1598), ed Charles Lethbridge Kingsford (Oxford: 1908), vol 1, p 39.

30 The experience described in a ballad quoted by John Orrell, *The Quest for Shakespeare's Globe* (Cambridge: 1983) p 45.

31 Stow, *A Survey of London*, vol 1, p 26.

32 *Measure for Measure*, I.ii.93.

33 *2 Henry IV*, III.ii.12.

34 Harrison's *Description of England* appeared as preface to Holinshed's *Chronicles* (1587).

35 Quoted in F P Wilson, *The Plague in Shakespeare's London* (Oxford: 1927) p 39.

36 Sir Philip Sidney, *An Apology for Poetry*, also called *The Defence of Poesy*, posthumously published 1595.

37 George or Richard Puttenham, *The Art of English Poesy* (1589). It is not known which of two brothers wrote this treatise.

38 Edmund Howes, quoted in Chambers, *Stage*, vol 2, p 373.

39 Chambers, *Stage*, vol 4, p 269.

40 Andrew Gurr, *The Shakespearean Stage* (Cambridge: 1970) p 51

41 The names *quarto* and *folio* are indications of size. In a
    quarto edition four pages of text were printed on each side
    of a sheet of paper, which was then folded twice to create
    eight pages of text. In a folio edition each sheet was folded
    once to create four pages of text.

42 By Walter Allen, *The English Novel* (Harmondsworth: 1954)
    p 21.

43 There is still debate about how much, in his early plays,
    Shakespeare worked in collaboration with other writers,
    Nashe for example. *Two Gentlemen* was one of the plays first
    published in the 1623 Folio (F).

44 The play we know as *The Taming of the Shrew* was first
    published in 1623 (F). However, a play with the slightly
    different title of *The Taming of a Shrew* was published in
    1594. The relationship between the two plays is unclear.
    Stanley Wells and Gary Taylor, with John Jowett and
    William Montgomery, *William Shakespeare, A Textual
    Companion* (Oxford: 1987) pp 109–11.

45 *Titus Andronicus* was first published in 1594, as a quarto
    edition (Q1).

46 Ted Hughes, *Tales from Ovid* (London: 1997) p viii.

47 A version of *2 Henry VI*, entitled *The First Part of the
    Contention betwixt the two Famous Houses of York and Lancaster*,
    was published in 1594. A version of *3 Henry VI*, entitled
    The True Tragedy of Richard Duke of York, was published in
    1595. *1 Henry VI* was not published until 1623 (F), and it
    may have been written last of the three (an early case of a
    hit followed by a prequel); but it is also possible that the
    three parts were written in the obvious order. They may
    have been written in collaboration.

48 Raphael Holinshed's *Chronicles of England, Scotland and
    Ireland* was first published in 1577. A second, expanded

edition appeared in 1587; several other writers, including Edmund Campion, contributed to it.

49 *Richard III* was first published in 1597 (Q1). The Folio version differs from Q1 in many ways.

50 For the Queen's reply Shakespeare uses the rhetorical device of *antanaclasis*, by which a word is picked up and used in a new sense. Puttenham, in his list of rhetorical figures, calls it the *Rebound*, 'alluding to the tennis ball which being smitten with the racket rebounds back again ... this playeth with one word written all alike but carrying divers senses' (*The Art of English Poesy*).

51 The Chettle passage is quoted in Chambers, *Stage*, vol 4, p 242. Nashe's disclaimer appeared in the second impression of his *Pierce Penniless his Supplication to the Devil* (1592).

52 Nashe, *Pierce Penniless*.

53 Chambers, *Stage*, vol 4, p 310.

54 Wilson, *The Plague in Shakespeare's London*.

55 Chambers, *Stage*, vol 4, p 301.

56 Thomas Dekker, *The Belman of London* (1608). Quoted in Chambers, *Stage*, vol 1, p 332

57 William Hazlitt, *The Characters of Shakespeare's Plays* (1817).

58 Richard Barnfield, *A Remembrance of some English Poets* (1598).

59 In 1599 versions of two sonnets (138, 144) were published, probably without authority, in a collection entitled *The Passionate Pilgrim*. Shakespeare was said to have been much offended. The whole set of Sonnets, together with *A Lover's Complaint*, was published by Thomas Thorpe in 1609, with a mysterious dedication to 'the only begetter' of the Sonnets, 'Mr W H'.

60 Francis Meres, *Palladis Tamia: Wit's Friend* (1598). It is possible that all the Sonnets were written by 1598, when

Meres referred to them; but they may have been written over a longer period. Many commentators believe that Sonnet 107 alludes to the Queen's death in 1603.

61 Quoted by C J Sisson in his 1934 British Academy Lecture, 'The Mythical Sorrows of Shakespeare', *Proceedings of the British Academy* (London) vol 20, p 49.

62 Frank Harris, *The Man Shakespeare and his Tragic Life-Story* (London: 1909) p 204.

63 Richard Barnfield, Sonnet 8, *Cynthia; with certain Sonnets* (1595).

64 *The Phoenix and the Turtle* was published in 1601, among the verses included with Robert Chester's long poem *Love's Martyr*. Wood, *In Search of Shakespeare*, pp 257–9, suggests that it might have been written in memory of the Catholic widow Anne Line, executed in 1601.

65 *The Comedy of Errors* was first published in 1623 (F).

66 Chambers, *Stage*, vol 4, p 56.

67 *Love's Labour's Lost* was first published in 1598 (Q1). This was the first time Shakespeare's name appeared on the title-page of a play.

68 S T Coleridge, *Notes and Lectures upon Shakespeare*, published posthumously in 1849.

69 Anonymous annotation in a copy of George Gascoigne's *Posies* (1575). *Elizabethan Critical Essays*, ed C Gregory Smith (Oxford: 1904) vol 1, p 360.

70 George C Odell, *Shakespeare – from Betterton to Irving* (New York: 1920) vol 2, pp 202f.

71 Chambers, *Stage*, vol 4, p 139.

72 Quoted in Edith Sitwell, *The Queens and the Hive* (London: 1962) p 413.

73 So described by Andrew Gurr in a lecture, 'Shakespeare and his Employers', at the National Portrait Gallery, 13 April 2006.

74 *The Return from Parnassus*, Part 2 (1601). Drayton, *Of Poets and Poesy*.

75 Chambers, *Stage*, vol 2, p 307.

76 Richard Flecknoe, *A Short Discourse of the English Stage* (1664).

77 *Romeo and Juliet* was first published in 1597 (Q1), an unreliable edition. The first authoritative edition appeared in 1599 (Q2). *A Midsummer Night's Dream* was first published in 1600 (Q1).

78 *Julius Caesar* V.iii.58; *Hamlet* V.ii.290; *Richard II* V.v.3; *Othello* V.ii.288.

79 Minor White Latham, *The Elizabethan Fairies* (New York: 1930).

80 *Richard II* was first published in 1597 (Q1).

81 *King John* was first published in 1623 (F).

82 Simon Forman, quoted by Harold F Brooks in his Arden edition of *A Midsummer Night's Dream* (London: 1979) p xxxvii.

83 Chambers, *Stage*, vol 4, p 318.

84 For instance, Wood, *In Search of Shakespeare*, p 199. Stephen Greenblatt, *Will in the World* (London: 2004) p 318, hereafter Greenblatt, *Will*.

85 Alfred Harbage wittily makes the point in an imaginary letter from Shakespeare to Hamnet Sadler. *Conceptions of Shakespeare* (Cambridge, Massachusetts: 1966) p 142.

86 Chambers, *Shakespeare*, vol 2, p 26.

87 Asa Briggs, *A Social History of England* (London: 1999) p 117, first published 1983.

88 This is the memory of a visitor who was born in 1683 and knew the house in his childhood. Chambers, *Shakespeare*, vol 2, p 99.

89 Schoenbaum, *Lives*, p 159.

90 Marchette Chute, *Shakespeare of London* (London: 1951) p 206.

91 *The Merchant of Venice* was first published in 1600 (Q1).

92 Quoted, in an eloquent passage, by Greenblatt, *Will*, p 277.

93 John Gross, *Shylock* (London: 1992).

94 Both plays were first published in quarto editions, *1 Henry IV* in 1598, *2 Henry IV* in 1600.

95 *The Merry Wives of Windsor* was first published in 1602 (Q1). The Folio version is longer.

96 *Much Ado About Nothing* was first published in 1600 (Q).

97 *Henry V* was first published in 1600 (Q1). The Folio version is longer and contains more patriotic material.

98 Jan Kott, *Shakespeare Our Contemporary*, translated by Boleslaw Taborski (London: 1964) p 5.

99 James Shapiro, *1599, A Year in the Life of William Shakespeare* (London: 2005) p 72

100 Chambers, *Shakespeare*, vol 2, pp 100, 102.

101 Chambers, *Stage*, vol 2, p 508.

102 Schoenbaum, *A Compact Documentary Life*, p 207.

103 Andrew Gurr, with John Orrell, *Rebuilding Shakespeare's Globe* (London: 1989). The authors explain the effect of the orientation of the Globe in relation to the sun (pp 22ff, 122f) and include illustrative photographs.

104 *Much Ado* III.i.24; *Julius Caesar* I.ii.187; *Othello* II.i.175.

105 John Orrell, *The Quest for Shakespeare's Globe* (Cambridge: 1983) p 140

106 *Julius Caesar* was first published in 1623 (F).

107 Harley Granville-Barker suggested Shakespeare's Romans could have looked something like the figures in Veronese's *Family of Darius* (National Gallery). It could almost be a picture of Cleopatra kneeling before Octavius – or perhaps Calpurnia pleading with Caesar. *Prefaces to Shakespeare* (London: 1958) vol 2, p 408. First published 1930.

108 Andrew Gurr, *Shakespeare's Hats* (Rome: 1993) pp 26, 34.

109 *As You Like It* was first published in 1623 (F).

110 Q1 of *Hamlet* (1603) is a corrupt text. Q2 (1604–05) is the first 'good' text, and it is 1,500 lines longer than Q1. The F version is shorter, but also contains passages not in Q2; these two good texts differ in many details. Some modern editions present a conflation of Q2 and F.

111 Chambers, *Shakespeare*, vol 2, pp 334f. There is an evocative description of this famous occasion in Wood, *In Search of Shakespeare*, pp 329f.

112 Sir Thomas Roe (1581?–1644). *The Raj*, ed Roger Hudson (London: 1999) p 5.

113 *Twelfth Night* was first published in 1623 (F).

114 Philip Stubbes, *The Anatomy of Abuses* (1583). Chambers, *Stage*, vol 4, pp 223f.

115 *Julius Caesar* IV.ii.320; *Much Ado* III.iii.57; *Twelfth Night* II.iv.20.

116 Quoted in J E Neale, *Queen Elizabeth I* (London: 1952) p 366. Originally published as *Queen Elizabeth* in 1934.

117 *Troilus and Cressida* was first published in 1609 (Q).

118 Simon Thurley, *The Royal Palaces of Tudor England* (New Haven and London: 1993) pp 28f.

119 Henry Chettle, *England's Mourning Garment* (1603).

120 Roy Strong, *Coronation* (London: 2005), pp 256, 261.

121 Thomas Nashe, Preface to Sidney's *Astrophil and Stella* (1591).

122 Ben Jonson, *His Part of King James his Royal and Magnificent Entertainment through his Honourable City of London* (1604).

123 The musician and autobiographer Thomas Whythorne (1528–96). Quoted in Liza Picard, *Elizabeth's London* (London: 2003) p 89.

124 *Measure for Measure* was first published in 1623 (F).

125 The treatise formed part of *The Essays of a Prentice in the Divine Art of Poesy*, printed in 1584, when James was 18 years old.

126 The story was one of the hundred tales in *Gli Hecatommithi* by Giraldi Cinthio (1565). The play was George Whetstone's *Promos and Cassandra* (1578).

127 *Othello* was first published in 1622 (Q1).

128 Wood, *In Search of Shakespeare*, pp 272–5, cites some moving examples.

129 Alison Sim, *Masters and Servants in Tudor England* (Stroud: 2006) pp 35ff.

130 Chambers, *Shakespeare*, vol 2, pp 90–5.

131 *All's Well That Ends Well* was first published in 1623 (F).

132 *Timon of Athens* was first published in 1623 (F). The arrangement of the volume suggests that it was included late, perhaps even as an afterthought.

133 For instance, Wood, *In Search of Shakespeare*, p 318.

134 Chambers, *Shakespeare*, vol 1, p 483.

135 *King Lear* was first published in 1608 (Q1). This version differs significantly from F, so much so that the Oxford editors include both versions in their edition of the Complete Works. Most modern editors offer a conflation of the two texts – probably unlike any version performed in Shakespeare's lifetime.

136 John L Murphy, *Darkness and Devils* (Athens, Ohio: 1984).

137 Charles Lamb, *On the Tragedies of Shakespeare, considered with reference to their fitness for stage representation* (1811).

138 *Macbeth* was first published in 1623 (F).

139 Sir James Fergusson of Kilkerran suggests that Shakespeare could have drawn on Lawrence Fletcher's first-hand knowledge of Scotland, in his *Shakespeare's Scotland* (Edinburgh: 1957).

140 Scholars have suspected cuts. There are interpolations too: the Hecate scene, a few lines elsewhere, and the songs specified in the stage directions are not by Shakespeare. The songs appear in Thomas Middleton's *The Witch*, written later than *Macbeth*; and it is possible that Middleton wrote the interpolated passages too; but Kenneth Muir, in his Arden *Macbeth* suggests that they were written by an anonymous poet in order to introduce the songs.

141 *Antony and Cleopatra* was first published in 1623 (F).

142 *Pericles* was first published in 1609 (Q1), a corrupt text. It was not included in F1, but was one of the seven plays newly included in the second impression of F3 (1664).

143 The Oxford editors argue that both the corrupt Q1 and Wilkins's prose novel should be regarded as memorial versions of the play.

144 *The Winter's Tale* V.ii.61; *Cymbeline* III.iv.92; *The Winter's Tale* III.i.7.

145 Ben Jonson, Induction to *Bartholomew Fair*, 1614; *Ode to Himself*, 1629?.

146 *Coriolanus* was first published in 1623 (F).

147 Kott, *Shakespeare Our Contemporary*, p 145.

148 The actor Jonathan Cake, preparing the part for performance in Shakespeare's Globe. Reported by Jasper Rees in 'Scrumming down for Coriolanus', *The Sunday Times*, 7 May 2006.

149 Chambers, *Shakespeare*, vol 2, p 214.

150 For instance, Wood (*In Search of Shakespeare*, p 281) writes that in 1603 Shakespeare was acting parts like John of Gaunt and Henry IV, as well as the Ghost.

151 All three plays were first published in 1623 (F).

152 The literary emancipation of Caliban has been going on for a long time, but in relatively recent years it has been given impetus by the cultural and political consciousness of Third

World writers and by the historical guilt of the liberal West. There is an interesting discussion in Ruby Cohn, *Modern Shakespeare Offshoots* (Princeton: 1976) Chapter 5.

153 Sir Francis Wyatt in 1622. Quoted in Simon Schama, *A History of Britain* (London: 2000) vol 1, p 408.

154 The word 'bastardized' comes from John Florio's translation of Montaigne's essay *Of the Cannibals* (1603). This essay, which celebrates the innocence of nature, was among Shakespeare's sources for the ideas of *The Tempest*.

155 *Henry VIII* was first published in 1623 (F), with no mention of Fletcher. *The Two Noble Kinsmen* was first published in 1634 (Q), attributed to Fletcher and Shakespeare. *Cardenio* was twice performed at court, 1612–13, and it was entered in the Stationers' Register in 1653 as by Fletcher and Shakespeare. Theobald claimed to have seen three manuscript copies, and in 1727 wrote his own version of the play.

156 Richard Buckle's 1964 Stratford Exhibition for the 400th anniversary of Shakespeare's birth included a miniature playhouse interior where 'the Traveller' could listen to recorded voices reciting beauties of Shakespeare. They included Wolsey's farewell, incomparably spoken by Ralph Richardson. The shade of Fletcher must have been pleased.

157 The view of Frank Kermode, *Shakespeare's Language* (London: 2000) p 312.

158 Ben Jonson, *Execration upon Vulcan*, written after the Fortune burned down in 1621.

159 Contemporary reports of the fire, including the ballad, are in Chambers, *Stage*, vol 2, pp 419–23.

160 Quoted in Chambers, *Stage*, vol 3, p 379.

161 Francis Bacon, *Of Masques and Triumphs*.

162 Ben Jonson, *An Expostulation with Inigo Jones* (1631).

163 Quoted in C Walter Hodges, *The Globe Restored* (London: 1953) pp 18, 22.

164 Conrad Russell, *The Crisis of Parliaments* (Oxford: 1971) pp 19f.

165 Eccles, *Warwickshire*, p 141.

166 Chambers, *Shakespeare*, vol 2, p 177.

167 Thomas Hiccox, for instance, refers in his will (1611) to the 'kind affection which I bear unto my beloved wife'. Jeanne Jones, *Family Life in Shakespeare's England* (Stroud: 1996) p 89.

168 On 23 February 2006 *The Daily Telegraph* reported the contention of Professor Hildegard Hammerschmidt-Hummel (Marburg and Mainz University) that Shakespeare died of lymph cancer; she claimed to have found in various portraits evidence of swelling near the left eye. The report added that the British scholarly reaction was not positive.

169 John Ward, Vicar of Stratford. Chambers, *Shakespeare*, vol 2, p 250

170 Charlton Hinman, Introduction to *The Norton Facsimile of the First Folio* (New York: 1968) p ix.

171 However, even in 1616 a stage writer was not always respected as a specialist professional. The earliest use of the word 'playwright' cited in OED is from 1687, an allusion to 'this damn'd Trade of a Play-wright'.

172 Anthony Burgess, *Shakespeare* (Harmondsworth: 1972) p 261; James Shapiro, *1599* (London: 2005) p viii; John Dover Wilson, *The Essential Shakespeare* (Cambridge: 1932) pp 5, 6, 8.

173 The Janssen, Droeshout and Chandos images, and five other portraits, are reproduced and discussed in Tarnya Cooper *et al*, *Searching for Shakespeare* (National Portrait Gallery, London: 2006).

174 Margaret Cavendish, Duchess of Newcastle, *Sociable Letters* (1664). *Shakespeare. The Critical Heritage*, vol 1, ed Brian Vickers (London: 1974) p 43.

175 Doctor Johnson's comment in the Preface to his edition of Shakespeare's Works, 1765.

176 Richard Wagner, *My Life*, Authorized Translation (London: 1911, 1944) p 36.

177 Chambers, *Shakespeare*, vol 2, pp 183f.

Year	Age	Life
1564		Birth of William, first son of John and Mary Shakespeare.
1566	2	Shakespeare's brother Gilbert born.
1568	4	John Shakespeare becomes Bailiff of Stratford.
1569	5	Shakespeare's sister Joan born.
1574	10	Shakespeare's brother Richard born.
1576	12	John Shakespeare in difficulties. James Burbage builds the Theatre.
1580	16	Shakespeare's brother Edmund born.
1582	18	Shakespeare marries Anne Hathaway.
1583	19	Shakespeare's daughter Susanna born.
1585	21	Shakespeare's twins Hamnet and Judith born.
1586	22	John Shakespeare resigns from the Stratford Corporation.

Year	History	Culture
1564	Peace of Troyes ends war between England and France.	Christopher Marlowe born.
1566	Murder of Mary Queen of Scot's secretary David Rizzio. Earl of Essex born.	Pieter Brueghel, 'St John the Baptist'.
1568	Mary Queen of Scots takes refuge in England.	Invention of bottled beer in London.
1569	Revolt of the Northern Earls in England.	Mercator's world map.
1574	Accession of Henry III of France.	Tintoretto, 'Paradiso', Doge's Palace, Venice.
1576	Philip II makes Don John of Austria governor of the Netherlands. Spanish sack Antwerp.	Death of Titian.
1580	Spanish invade Portugal. Ivan the Terrible kills his own son.	Montaigne, *Essais*.
1582	James VI of Scotland seized by Protestant nobles.	Hakluyt, *Divers Voyages Touching the Discovery of America*.
1583	James VI of Scotland escapes his captors. Throgmorton Plot against Elizabeth I.	Queen's Company of Players formed in London.
1585	Sir Francis Drake attacks Vigo and Santo Domingo.	Death of French poet Ronsard.
1586	Babington Plot against Elizabeth I revealed: Mary Queen of Scots implicated and later executed.	Death of Sir Philip Sidney.

Year	Age	Life
1592	28	Robert Greene attacks Shakespeare. Henry Chettle apologises.
1593	29	Publication of *Venus and Adonis*, dedicated to Southampton.
1594	30	*The Rape of Lucrece*, dedicated to Southampton. Shakespeare a member of the Company of the Chamberlain's Men. *Titus Andronicus. 2 Henry VI.*
1595	31	*3 Henry VI.*
1596	32	Death of Hamnet. Grant of Arms to John Shakespeare. James Burbage acquires the Blackfriars hall. The Swan playhouse in use
1597	33	Shakespeare buys New Place. *Richard III. Richard II.*
1598	34	The Theatre dismantled. *Love's Labour's Lost. 1 Henry IV.*
1599	35	The Globe built. *Romeo and Juliet* (Q2).
1600	36	Birth of William, first son of Shakespeare's sister Joan, by now married to William Hart. *A Midsummer Night's Dream. The Merchant of Venice. 2 Henry IV. Much Ado About Nothing. Henry V.*
1601	37	Death of John Shakespeare. *The Phoenix and the Turtle.*
1602	38	Shakespeare buys land in Old Stratford and the Chapel Lane cottage. *The Merry Wives of Windsor*
1603	39	The Chamberlain's Men become the King's Men.

Year	History	Culture
1592	Plague kills thousands in London.	Thomas Kyd, *The Spanish Tragedy*.
1593	Henry IV of France converts to Catholicism.	Christopher Marlowe killed.
1594	Henry IV of France enters Paris.	Death of Thomas Kyd.
1595	Spanish raid on Cornwall.	Death of Italian poet Tasso.
1596	English sack Cadiz.	Spenser, *The Faerie Queen* Books 4–6.
1597	Second Spanish Armada dispersed by storms.	James VI of Scotland, *Daemonologie* (on witches).
1598	Edict of Nantes grants French Huguenots freedom of worship.	Ben Jonson, *Every Man in His Humour*.
1599	Earl of Essex arrested on return from Ireland for unauthorised truce with rebels.	James VI of Scotland, *Basilikon Doron* (on kingship).
1600	Earl of Essex stripped of court offices.	Caravaggio, 'Doubting Thomas'.
1601	Essex's rebellion: Essex later executed.	Ben Jonson, *The Poetaster*.
1602	Spanish army lands in Ireland; surrenders at Kinsale.	
1603	Death of Elizabeth I: accession of James VI of Scotland as James I of England.	Monteverdi, 'Fourth Book of Madrigals'.

Year	Age	Life
1604	40	Shakespeare helps arrange the Mountjoy-Belott marriage. *Hamlet* (Q2)
1605	41	Shakespeare invests in Stratford tithes.
1607	43	Susanna Shakespeare marries John Hall. Death of Edmund Shakespeare.
1608	44	Birth of Shakespeare's granddaughter Elizabeth. Death of Mary Shakespeare. The King's Men take over the Blackfriars playhouse. *King Lear*.
1609	45	*The Sonnets. Troilus and Cressida. Pericles.*
1612	48	The Mountjoy-Belott case. Death of Gilbert Shakespeare.
1613	49	Death of Richard Shakespeare. Shakespeare buys the Blackfriars Gatehouse. The Globe burns down.
1614	50	The Second Globe in use. Enclosures dispute begins.
1616	52	Judith Shakespeare marries Thomas Quiney. Quiney summoned to the Church Court. Death of William Hart. Death of William Shakespeare.

Year	History	Culture
1604	Peace between England and Spain.	Sir Francis Bacon, *The Advancement of Learning*.
1605	The Gunpowder Plot.	Cervantes, *Don Quixote* Part I.
1607	Union of England and Scotland rejected by English Parliament.	Monteverdi, opera 'Orfeo'.
1608	Collapse of O'Doherty rebellion in Ireland. Galileo invents astronomical telescope.	Birth of John Milton.
1609	Twelve years truce between Spain and the United Provinces.	
1612	Death of Henry, Prince of Wales.	El Greco, 'Baptism of Christ'.
1613	Elizabeth, daughter of James I, marries Frederick V of the Palatinate.	Guido Reni, 'Aurora' frescoes in Rome.
1614	James I dissolves his second Parliament.	Ben Jonson, *Bartholomew Fayre*.
1616	James I starts to sell peerages to raise money.	First folio edition of Ben Jonson's works published.

Chronology of Plays

The chronology of composition for Shakespeare's plays, as suggested in the Oxford *Textual Companion*, is as follows:

1590–1	*The Two Gentlemen of Verona, The Taming of the Shrew*
1591	*2 Henry VI, 3 Henry VI*
1592	*1 Henry VI, Titus Andronicus*
1592–3	*Richard III*
1594	*The Comedy of Errors*
1594–5	*Love's Labour's Lost*
1595	*Richard II, Romeo and Juliet, A Midsummer Night's Dream*
1596	*King John*
1596–7	*The Merchant of Venice, 1 Henry IV*
1597–8	*The Merry Wives of Windsor, 2 Henry IV*
1598	*Much Ado About Nothing*
1598–9	*Henry V*
1599	*Julius Caesar*
1599–1600	*As You Like It*
1600–01	*Hamlet*
1601	*Twelfth Night*
1602	*Troilus and Cressida*
1603	*Measure for Measure*
1603–04	*Othello*
1604–05	*All's Well That Ends Well*

Further Reading

Shakespeare's Works

The giant among available editions is *The Oxford Shakespeare* (1986, 2005) under the general editorship of Stanley Wells and Gary Taylor. It is magnificently comprehensive and full of surprises; the second edition offers even more pleasures, including full texts of *Sir Thomas More* and *Edward III*, and a helpful bibliography. For those who prefer a more conventional text, the well-loved Peter Alexander edition (Collins) is still available, revised (1994), with accompanying essays by Anthony Burgess and Germaine Greer. The admirable *Arden Shakespeare* presents each play in a separate volume, with very full critical and textual notes; it is now well into its 3rd edition. *The New Penguin Shakespeare* also presents separate volumes, with short and helpful notes and scholarly introductions – perfect for use on the stage; a new edition began in 2005.

Books about Shakespeare

The literature about Shakespeare is huge and still growing. Most of the books in this very brief selection were published quite recently, and all are still easy to find.

Ackroyd, Peter, *Shakespeare: The Biography* (London: 2005).
Bate, Jonathan, *The Genius of Shakespeare* (London: 1997).
Chute, Marchette, *Shakespeare of London* (London: 1951).

Coghill, Nevill, *Shakespeare's Professional Skills* (Cambridge: 1964).

Cooper, Tarnya *et al*, *Searching for Shakespeare* (London: 2006).

Crystal, David and Ben, *Shakespeare's Words* (London: 2002).

Devlin, Christopher, *Hamlet's Divinity* (London: 1963).

Dobson, Michael, and Stanley Wells (eds), *The Oxford Companion to Shakespeare* (Oxford: 2001)

Duncan-Jones, Katherine, *Ungentle Shakespeare: Scenes from his Life* (London: 2001).

Foakes, R A, *Henslowe's Diary* (Cambridge: 1961, 2002).

Gillespie, Stuart, *Shakespeare's Books* (London: 2001).

Greenblatt, Stephen, *Will in the World* (London: 2004).

Gurr, Andrew, *The Shakespearean Stage 1574-1642* (Cambridge: 1970, 1992).

——, *Playgoing in Shakespeare's London* (Cambridge: 1987, 2004).

——, *The Shakespeare Company 1594-1642* (Cambridge: 2004).

——, and John Orrell, *Rebuilding Shakespeare's Globe* (London: 1989).

Halliday, F E, *The Life of Shakespeare* (London: 1961).

Harbage, Alfred, *Shakespeare's Audience* (New York: 1941).

——, *Conceptions of Shakespeare* (Cambridge, Massachusetts: 1966).

Hodges, C Walter, *The Globe Restored* (London: 1953).

Honan, Park, *Shakespeare, a Life* (Oxford: 1998).

Honigmann, E A J, *Shakespeare: The Lost Years* (Manchester: 1985, 1998).

Kermode, Frank, *Shakespeare's Language* (London: 2000).

——, *The Age of Shakespeare* (London: 2004).

Muir, Kenneth, *The Sources of Shakespeare's Plays* (London: 1977).

Palmer, Alan and Veronica, *Who's Who in Shakespeare's England* (London: 1981).

Schoenbaum, S, *Shakespeare's Lives* (Oxford: 1970, 1991).

Schoenbaum, S, *William Shakespeare, A Compact Documentary Life* (Oxford: 1977).

Shapiro, James, *1599, A Year in the Life of William Shakespeare* (London: 2005).

Styan, J L, *Shakespeare's Stagecraft* (Cambridge: 1967).

——, *The English Stage* (Cambridge: 1996).

Wells, Stanley, *Shakespeare: A Dramatic Life* (London: 1994).

——, and Gary Taylor, with John Jowett and William Montgomery, *William Shakespeare: A Textual Companion* (Oxford: 1987).

——, and James Shaw, *A Dictionary of Shakespeare* (Oxford: 1998).

Wood, Michael, *In Search of Shakespeare* (London: 2003).

Picture Sources

The author and publishers wish to express their thanks to the following sources of illustrative material and/or permission to reproduce it. They will make the proper acknowledgements in future editions in the event that any omissions have occurred.

Topham Picturepoint: pp. iii, 9, 23, 32–3, 42, 54, 76, 84, 106, 113, 120, 147.

Index

All family relationships are to William Shakespeare.
For Shakespeare's works, see under Shakespeare, William.

H

Hall, Elizabeth
  (granddaughter), 135
Hall, John (son-in-law), 135,
  169
Harington, Sir John, 55
Harrison, John, 55
Harrison, William, 39, 84
Harsnett, Samuel, 130–1
Hart, Michael (nephew), 143
Hart, William (brother-in-
  law), 112
Hart, William Jnr. (nephew),
  112
Harvey, Gabriel, 66
Harvey, Sir William, 59
Hathaway, Anne (wife), 22–6,
  130, 144, 148, 159–60,
  162
Hathaway, Bartholomew
  (brother-in-law), 24, 28, 39
Hathaway, Francis, 26
Hathaway, Richard (father-in-
  law), 24, 148
Haydn, Joseph, 111
Heminges, John, 28, 73, 74,
  99, 142, 157, 159
Henry, Prince of Wales, 151
Henry VIII, King, 69
Henslowe, Philip, 39, 51, 68,
  70, 108
Hesketh, Sir Thomas, 16
Heywood, Thomas, 73

Hiccox, Lewis, 144
Hoghton, Alexander, 15
Howard of Effingham, Lord,
  68

I

Irving, Sir Henry, 3

J

James I, King, 116, 117–19,
  121, 132, 144
Janssen, Gheerart, 162
Jenkins, Thomas, 9
Johnson, Samuel, 39
Jones, Davy, 26
Jones, Inigo, 124, 155
Jones, Robert, 111
Jonson, Ben, 38, 97, 108,
  118, 124, 140, 145, 149,
  164, 165, 169

K

Keeling, Captain William,
  109–10
Kempe, William, 70, 74, 93,
  99, 106
Knell, William, 27
Kyd, Thomas, 42–3, 71

L

Lane, John, 158
Langley, Francis, 86
Lanier, Emilia, 59, 89